bar
Encountering Jesus in Revelation

Encountering Jesus in Revelation

The Apocalyptic Perspective That Calls Us to Follow the Lamb

BEN BOECKEL

WIPF & STOCK · Eugene, Oregon

ENCOUNTERING JESUS IN REVELATION
The Apocalyptic Perspective That Calls Us to Follow the Lamb

Copyright © 2024 Ben Boeckel. All rights reserved. Except for brief quotations in critical publications or reviews, no part of this book may be reproduced in any manner without prior written permission from the publisher. Write: Permissions, Wipf and Stock Publishers, 199 W. 8th Ave., Suite 3, Eugene, OR 97401.

Wipf & Stock
An Imprint of Wipf and Stock Publishers
199 W. 8th Ave., Suite 3
Eugene, OR 97401

www.wipfandstock.com

PAPERBACK ISBN: 979-8-3852-1232-3
HARDCOVER ISBN: 979-8-3852-1233-0
EBOOK ISBN: 979-8-3852-1234-7

02/05/24

Unless otherwise indicated, Scripture quotations are taken from the (NASB®) New American Standard Bible®, Copyright © 2020 by The Lockman Foundation. Used by permission. All rights reserved. lockman.org

Scripture quotations marked (NIV) are taken from the Holy Bible, New International Version®, NIV®. Copyright © 1973, 1978, 1984, 2011 by Biblica, Inc.™ Used by permission of Zondervan. All rights reserved worldwide. www.zondervan.com The "NIV" and "New International Version" are trademarks registered in the United States Patent and Trademark Office by Biblica, Inc.™

Scripture quotations marked (ESV) are taken from the ESV® Bible (The Holy Bible, English Standard Version®), © 2001 by Crossway, a publishing ministry of Good News Publishers. Used by permission. All rights reserved. The ESV text may not be quoted in any publication made available to the public by a Creative Commons license. The ESV may not be translated in whole or in part into any other language.

Scripture quotations from The Authorized (King James) Version. Rights in the Authorized Version in the United Kingdom are vested in the Crown. Reproduced by permission of the Crown's patentee, Cambridge University Press.

To Peter and Hannah:
May you always follow the Lamb.

Contents

List of Tables		ix
Acknowledgments		xi
Abbreviations		xiii
Introduction		xv
1	What Kind of Book Is Revelation?	1
2	Eschatology and Apocalyptic Literature	11
3	A Revelation	20
4	Letters to the Churches	28
5	Heavenly Worship	45
6	The Seals	56
7	The Trumpets	71
8	Anticipating the Kingdom's Arrival	85
9	Worship Wars	99
10	Outpouring God's Justice	118
11	Babylon's Demise	130
12	Touring the New Creation	147
13	Epilogue	172
Appendix A: The Shepherd of Hermas: Excerpts from Visions 3–4		175
Bibliography		185

List of Tables

1. Jesus' Letters to the Seven Churches
2. Similarities Between the Scrolls of Revelation 10 and Ezekiel 2
3. Parallels Between the Sixth Bowl and Sixth Trumpet

Acknowledgments

This book began while I taught a Wednesday evening Bible study on Revelation at the Grangeville Church of the Nazarene. I am grateful for the feedback and the lively conversations we had as the body of Christ in that upstairs fellowship hall. During these evenings, Revelation did what it so often does: it challenged and comforted us over the year and a half of our study.

    I am also grateful to Jack Levison who put me in touch with the wonderful people at Wipf and Stock and in doing so motivated me to finish editing the first draft of this book. Lastly, I am grateful to Pastor Chris Galloway who read a rough draft of several of these chapters and provided valuable feedback and insight.

Abbreviations

Bible Versions

CEB   Common English Bible. Nashville: The Common English Bible, 2011.

ESV   English Standard Version. Wheaton: Crossway, 2016.

LXX   The Septuagint, the Greek translation of the Old Testament.

NASB   New American Standard Bible. La Habra: Lockman Foundation, 2020.

NIV   New International Version. Grand Rapids: Zondervan, 2011.

NRSV   New Revised Standard Version. Nashville: Thomas Nelson, 1989.

Scholarly Sources

ANF   *The Ante-Nicene Fathers*. Edited by Alexander Roberts et al. 10 vols. New York: Christian Literature Company, 1885–87.

EncJud   *Encyclopedia Judaica*. Edited by Fred Skolnik and Michael Berenbaum. 2nd ed. 22 vols. Detroit: Macmillan Reference USA, 2007.

LSJ   Liddell, Henry George, Robert Scott, and Henry Stuart Jones. *A Greek-English Lexicon*. 9th ed. With revised supplement. Oxford: Clarendon, 1996.

Introduction

"I'm sick of adventures!"[1] These words, spoken in C. S. Lewis's *The Silver Chair*, capture the angst of anyone swept up in an adventure. Adventure stories immerse readers in all the challenges and conflicts experienced in the course of good triumphing over evil. For that reason, they are exciting. But Lewis's words capture another quality of any adventure (fictional and non-fictional alike): very little of it is enjoyable in the moment.

Imagine a book that narrates the adventure of a people struggling to survive while awaiting deliverance and simultaneously invites its readers to live as that people. That is what the book of Revelation accomplishes. It invites the church to await the return of Jesus with anticipation even as monsters, demons, and nations try to snuff out the existence of God's people. Revelation is a thrilling read and sometimes scary once we hear Jesus' call to enter the story.

This book attempts to equip Christians to hear anew the story of Revelation and its message to the church through the centuries. To accomplish this, we shall situate Revelation within its historical context—considering how it addressed its first audiences—while also positioning ourselves to receive the challenges and encouragements Revelation poses to the church. Of course, many authors have attempted this; some have succeeded.

I wrote this study after I began to preach and teach Revelation in a congregation in rural Idaho. As I engaged Revelation, I discovered a dearth of resources that (1) suited the needs of church leaders and (2) possessed the requisite depth for reading Revelation responsibly. Many of the resources available are high-altitude overviews that do not address the details of the text, or they are written by pastors for pastors and lack credibility afforded

1. Lewis, *Silver Chair*, 63.

by advanced training in biblical studies. Of course, there are top-notch academic publications available, but most pastors lack the training to use these in meaningful ways (let alone the funds to purchase them). In this book, I utilized those tools to assist pastors and lay leaders in reading the text of Revelation faithfully. If this study can encourage an otherwise trepidatious church leader to engage Revelation and to lead others into its pages for an encounter with Jesus' message for his bride, then I will have accomplished what I set out to do in publishing this book.

The following pages dive deeper than most studies attempting to make Revelation accessible to laypeople. At the same time, neither have I written as a scholar for scholars. This book threads the needle between those two poles: speaking to readers without presuming formal education in biblical studies while also reaping the fruits biblical scholarship has to offer.

As we approach the study of Revelation, I would commend to readers three principles of interpretation. First, read Revelation humbly. The contentiousness that surrounds Revelation in the church has less to do with its contents and more to do with the pride of its readers. If we remain humble, we shall better position ourselves to hear the unpretentious call of Christ within our world. In any case, saying, "This is what I think, but I could be wrong" has helped me maintain fellowship with those who read Revelation differently than I do. Remember, the Christian faith affirms the inspiration *of Scripture*, not of one's understanding of a particular text. For the most part, the meaning of symbols in Revelation does not involve the core confessions of the Christian faith (e.g., that Christ shall return and the dead shall be raised). As such, there is room for humble disagreement regarding the symbolism of Revelation.

Second, read the final book of the Bible with one eye on the text of Revelation and the other eye on the Old Testament. In my graduate studies, I specialized in Old Testament and that training has convinced me that Revelation draws unceasingly on the Scriptures of Israel, especially the book of Exodus. Regretfully, many readers, even scholarly ones, overlook the influence of books like Exodus and what these might contribute to a reading of Revelation. In the pages to follow, I endeavor to rectify that oversight.

Finally, read Revelation with attention to its main themes. As we journey through the Scripture, we will encounter three major themes recurring in Revelation. Perhaps the most fundamental theme in Revelation is worship; Revelation is about worship. Specifically, it engages the question of who is worthy of worship and insists that the answer is Christ alone. Of course, others vie for this position in our lives, and that is one of the realities that Revelation reveals.

Another theme is the two-sided nature of reality. Apocalyptic literature fixates on both the physical world that we see and the spiritual reality we often overlook. Revelation alternates between pictures of chaos on earth and glimpses of creation rightly ordered in heaven. This dual-focus speaks to the people of God in the "now," whenever "now" might be. It depicts our life and struggles on a cosmic scale and reminds us of the hope of the Christian faith: Jesus is coming soon!

A final theme that warrants mention here is exodus—the event and the book. As mentioned above, the book of Exodus plays an important role in Revelation. This is especially observable with the trumpet and bowl judgments that exhibit substantial resonance with the plagues of Egypt. However, the influence of Exodus runs even deeper since Revelation offers the invitation of Christ to leave behind our world and join him on the heavenly side of the glassy sea. In this new exodus, we encounter Jesus and life with him.

With these three interpretive tools—a posture humility, knowledge of the Old Testament, and an eye on the central themes of Revelation—we may begin our study. The chapters that follow will acquaint us with the kind of writing Revelation is (chapters 1–2) and then walk through the message of Revelation itself (chapters 3–12).

Before we proceed, some special notes are in order: first, when quoting Scripture, I have endeavored to identify the source of the translations used. When no translation is specified, it derives from the 2020 edition of the New American Standard Bible. Throughout the study, I routinely employ my own translations of Scripture and these are cited as such.

Secondly, throughout the study, I follow Rev 5 in identifying Jesus as the Lamb. As a title for Jesus, this is capitalized throughout the book. However, when specifically speaking about the metaphor of the lamb used in Revelation 5 and related texts, I do not capitalize "lamb."

Thirdly, within biblical studies and the academy at large, there is much thought regarding whether and which English pronouns should refer to God. Because I consider it poor English style to use words like "God, Godself, etc." repeatedly within the span of a couple of sentences, I have elected to use pronouns for God. I have also followed the practice of biblical writers by employing masculine pronouns for God, while acknowledging that the Triune God of the Christian faith transcends gender and that both men and women share equally in God's image. Besides stylistic concerns, I use masculine pronouns for God because the linguist in me refuses to surrender to theologians who commit the category error of conflating biological gender with grammatical gender. The English noun "God" is grammatically masculine (just as "goddess" is grammatically feminine) and grammar requires pronouns to follow the suit of their antecedents. Thus, an English speaker referring to God as "he" is no more a biological statement than any other time a linguistic user matches the gender of a pronoun to that of its referent.

Finally, regarding the author of Revelation, there is scholarly debate on the identity of the "John" identified in Rev 1:1. Was he one of Jesus' twelve apostles? Was he someone else of the same name? Was he the author of the fourth gospel? Is the book pseudonymous? Because the issue makes little difference for interpreting of the message of Revelation, I have intentionally made no claims here, though I do believe Revelation exhibits some consistency with other so-called Johannine literature in the New Testament. For pragmatic purposes, I assume a late first-century date for the writing of Revelation and refer to its author as "John" since that is how he identified himself (Rev 22:8).

1

What Kind of Book Is Revelation?

1. Introduction

For all the thrill that Revelation can offer readers as it addresses the church throughout history, it is also a lost treasure in the lives of many Christians. Revelation offers important challenges and comforts to followers of Jesus, but many of us seldom receive these gifts due to a number of factors. Leaders in the church frequently give the final book in the Bible a wide berth because it is difficult to understand and many recognize they are unequipped to read it responsibly. The church also fails to hear the message of Revelation when its reading becomes hijacked by different theories about the end times. While such theories create fascinating speculations that spark our imaginations, they also engender controversies and can create factions within the body of Christ. This is another reason many pastors and Bible study leaders avoid Revelation.

When that happens, however, the monsters of Revelation claim victory. When the church is too afraid—or unequipped—to hear the words of Scripture, she loses out on what the Spirit says to the churches. The purpose of this study is to reclaim Revelation from its relative obscurity and to allow it to speak afresh to God's people. Our objective is to equip readers to understand the message of Revelation by giving due attention to what it communicated in the first century and how that message resonates in new ways twenty-one centuries later.

With that goal in mind, we must address a preliminary matter: before diving into a book like Revelation, we need to know what it is that we are reading. Revelation is unlike other books in the Bible in that it employs types of writing that are particularly unfamiliar to most English readers. Consequently, our first task is to consider the form, or genre, of Revelation.

Revelation blends several different forms of writing. It is a letter to seven churches in Asia Minor. It also contains prayers, hymns, doxologies, blessings, and curses. Each of these could occupy much of our time as they point to a central theme in Revelation: worship. Even so, there are four forms of writing that dominate the book and therefore warrant our attention here: letter, prophecy, eschatology, and apocalypse.

2. Letter

Perhaps the most familiar form of writing we encounter in Revelation is its use of letters. John wrote Revelation on the island of Patmos as a pastoral letter to seven churches in the Roman province of Asia (modern day Turkey). Consequently, Revelation served a similar function to Paul's letters. Pastoral letters were how the apostles communicated with churches when they were geographically distant.

In the case of Revelation, the letter was sent to churches located in a regional hub for the imperial cult. Even when the larger Roman world was not engaged in active persecution of Christians, this part of the empire remained zealous about its religious traditions. This was especially the case in cities like Ephesus, where the temple of Artemis was one of the seven wonders of the ancient world, and Pergamum with its colossal altar for Zeus.

The epistolary nature (letter format) of Revelation appears mostly in chapters 2–3, where John records messages from Jesus to the seven churches. As messages from Jesus to his people, they also acquire a prophetic quality (see below). Additionally, the letters introduce the central vision of Rev 4–5 and thereby impact how one will understand the content of John's visions. If the reader identifies with the church of Philadelphia (to whom Jesus issued no threats or warnings), Revelation will be filled with hope. By contrast, if one finds him or herself in Laodicea, the visions of Revelation are a wake-up call urging one to repent and become faithful to Christ. With such a wake-up call, we are very close already to the next form of writing we encounter in Revelation.

3. Prophecy

Perhaps the most readily visible aspect of Revelation is its prophetic character. Indeed, it is the climax of the biblical prophetic tradition. The hopes anticipated by Israel's prophets reach their culmination here. Israel's prophetic tradition involved much more than what contemporary Western readers imagine when we think of prophecy.

Our understanding of prophecy arises more from Hollywood than Scripture. In the United States, people tend to associate prophecy with old (or ancient) writings that cryptically predict events in the distant future from the perspective of the prophecy's author. This conception of prophecy reduces the prophet to a fortune teller—a clairvoyant who possesses the ability to know things beforehand.

It is crucial for students of Scripture to recognize that, while this view of prophecy has ancient precedents, it is not the view of prophecy one finds in Scripture. In the Old Testament (and the New Testament), the prophet's role was first and foremost to stand before God's people proclaiming, "Thus says the LORD . . ."

This message could take various forms depending on the situation. Often, the message came as a call to return to God when the people had wandered astray. Typically, alongside a call to repentance, the proclamation included a warning if the people refused to repent. Like all warnings, those of prophecy included a predictive element: "If you do not turn back, then God will do such and such." Other times, when God's people were faithful but under threat—whether spiritual or political—the prophetic message arrived as a call to remain faithful and trust in the God who would ultimately deliver.

Revelation deploys both forms of prophecy simultaneously. Churches in places like Smyrna and Philadelphia (Rev 2–3), where Jesus apparently found nothing requiring correction, could hear hope in Revelation's call to overcome in the midst of trials. By contrast, churches like Sardis (the church that thinks it is alive, but is dead) and Laodicea (the lukewarm church) found in Revelation a call to repentance and warnings of destruction if they failed to overcome by following Jesus faithfully.

As one who wrote within Israel's prophetic tradition, John also drew on imagery throughout the Old Testament. He employed pictures and symbols to convey his prophetic message to the church. Consequently, readers of Revelation hear many echoes from books like Ezekiel, Zechariah, Daniel, and Jeremiah. But John did not limit himself to those books. Revelation also draws on the larger story of Israel—especially the exodus—as it beckons the church to follow the Lamb. As prophecy, the point of John's imagery and symbolism is to comfort those afflicted in the church and to afflict those who are too comfortable.

4. Eschatology and Apocalypse

In addition to prophecy, two additional terms that describe Revelation are "eschatology" and "apocalypse." These terms are related, but distinct from one another. Eschatology is a broad category of thought and reflection on the end times whereas apocalypse is a specific form of writing.

Eschatology may take many literary forms (genres). It may be conveyed through prose, poetry, epistles, apocalypses, and even theology textbooks. In the Old Testament, eschatology took various forms ranging from the hope for God's fulfillment of his promises to Abraham's descendants to a hope for the restoration of the kingdom of Israel under an heir to David's throne. Both of these hopes predated the development of apocalyptic literature. Although Israel's early (preexile) reflections on eschatology included both God's judgment and deliverance, there was very little that resembled the cosmic showdowns between good and evil that arise in apocalyptic writings.

Apocalyptic literature is a specific form of writing that encourages reflection on God's eschatological salvation. As such, we might say that all apocalyptic literature is eschatological, but not every text that addresses eschatology is apocalyptic. Apocalyptic writing developed relatively lately in comparison to other genres. It was popular in the centuries immediately preceding and following the earthly ministry of Jesus. The only example of fully developed apocalyptic literature in the Old Testament is Dan 7–12. By the end of the first century CE, however, examples of apocalyptic writing abound. This is where we find the book of Revelation. In addition to being prophecy and eschatology, Revelation is apocalyptic.

Revelation is one instance of many examples of the type of writing called "apocalypse." Just as modern readers readily recognize there are many examples of news articles in our time that come from different publishers (CNN, MSNBC, Fox News, not to mention the hundreds of local news stations), there were many apocalypses in the first century from a variety of sources. This comparison might help us understand an important difficulty modern readers experience when attempting to make sense of Revelation.

Whereas Western readers are well-versed in how to read or watch the news, most of us have read nothing like Revelation. In other words, because of the abundance of news media, a modern reader can move seamlessly between different news websites (or channels). We are familiar with the form of writing and we experience no struggle in understanding the meaning of the text—even if it reports from a perspective with which we disagree, or uses analogies that are foreign to us. But imagine your great grandmother, who never experienced reading a news article on a phone or computer. As she scrolled through a news story and came across an ad on the website (whether on the sidebar or something in the middle of the news story), she might be confused as to how it related to the rest of the article. It would be a major stumbling block to her understanding of the story.

That is the exact stumbling block modern readers encounter with Revelation. Because we are unfamiliar with type of media we are reading (apocalypse), we experience difficulty in areas that first-century readers would have grasped intuitively. Consequently, before jumping into the text of Revelation, it will greatly assist us if we spend some time exploring apocalyptic literature as a form of writing.

5. Exploring Apocalyptic Literature

The word "apocalypse" means "revelation." Thus, apocalyptic (or, revelatory) writing conveys an otherworldly revelation to its readers. The book of Revelation begins with the Greek words *apokalypsis Iesou Christou*, "a revelation of Jesus Christ." In other words, the content of the revelation is Jesus. The book reveals the truth about Jesus' identity and that of his followers. Of course, Jesus is not only the revelation's content, he is also the one who does the revealing (Rev 1:1).

For this revelation of Jesus to be meaningful to us, we must be able to understand the media that conveys it to us. So, *how* is the revelation transmitted to us? What does it mean to call Revelation *apocalyptic literature*? John Collins, a prominent Old Testament scholar, has defined "apocalyptic literature" as the following:

> A genre of revelatory literature within a narrative framework, in which a revelation is mediated by an otherworldly being to a human recipient, disclosing a transcendent reality which is both

temporal, insofar as it envisages eschatological salvation, and spatial insofar as it involves another, supernatural world.[1]

Although it is long and complex, this definition offers an excellent description that includes many components of the type of writing we find in Revelation. First, Revelation has a narrative framework. Unlike standalone prophetic oracles of salvation or destruction in Isaiah or Amos, Revelation's prophecy appears within a larger story of Jesus revealing himself to John and the church.

John tells the story of his receipt of this revelation from Jesus (Rev 1:9–20). Further, in line with Collins's definition, the reality Jesus disclosed to John was both temporal and spatial. It was temporal in that the revelation anticipated God's eschatological (end of time) salvation. It was also spatial in that what John saw in his visions pertained not only to our physical world, but also provided a glimpse into heaven itself as he watched worship services and judgments proclaimed there.

As mentioned before, Revelation is not the only book that exhibits these characteristics. Other influential (non-biblical) apocalypses from the ancient world include 1 Enoch (third century BCE), 4 Ezra (first century CE), the Apocalypse of Peter (second century CE), and the Shepherd of Hermas (also second century CE), which we will discuss in the chapter 2.

For now, several additional characteristics of apocalyptic writing warrant our consideration if we are to understand Revelation as an apocalypse.

Dualism

If we were to understand history as a play at the theater, we might say that one characteristic of apocalyptic writing is that it moves the venue from a hole-in-the-wall theater to a cosmic stage. No longer are we talking about Jerusalem and Rome. Apocalyptic writings give us heaven and hell engaged in epic battles. The purpose for this is to assist us as readers to understand our place in the midst of a struggle between good and evil, between God and the devil, between followers of God on the one hand and those who reject God on the other hand. With such extremes, apocalyptic writing naturally includes what one writer has dubbed an "ethical dualism" in which

---

1. Collins, "Introduction," 9.

each individual must choose a side, whether that is with God and the good, or with evil and Satan.[2]

Revelation certainly portrays a struggle and a choice to its readers, but this is also a place where it departs from other examples of apocalyptic writing. The dualism in Revelation is not a true dualism because the battle is already won. The crucified Jesus already reigns victorious as the slaughtered Lamb who sits on the throne. Granted, we do not always perceive his rule on this side of eternity. Often it appears that evil is winning, but Revelation is clear: God is making all things new and has already won the victory. Thus, Jesus speaks with royal and divine authority to the churches in Rev 2–3.

Symbols

If anything can be agreed upon regarding Revelation, it is that symbols abound. Revelation is filled with symbols. It is a vivid book that is stuffed to the brim with imagery.

While that imagery adds to the beauty of Revelation, the use of symbol also complicates its interpretation. Symbols are rich with meaning and often exhibit multiple meanings. Consider the debate surrounding the Confederate flag in the United States of America. In 2020, the state of Mississippi's legislature voted to remove the Confederate battle emblem from its state flag. The reason was that the emblem is a symbol that conveys a meaning that many associate with the glorification of national racism and oppression.

Of course, the change was also vehemently opposed. Many Mississippians cherished their state flag and their state history, warts and all. For them, the issue was not one of racism as much as the importance of remembering the past. For these people, that past—along with all the good the state has accomplished in the past one hundred years—was also symbolized by the flag.

What we see here is that different groups of people find different meaning in the same symbol. This happens in Revelation as well. Symbols carry different meanings for different readers. Sometimes this is by design. In Rev 17, the seven heads of the scarlet beast simultaneously represent seven hills and seven kings (Rev 17:9–10). Sometimes, the significance of the symbol is in the eye of the beholder. Thus, the faithful church rejoices and praises the Lamb as savior (Rev 7:10), but others are terrified by the wrath of the Lamb (6:16–17).

2. Gorman, *Reading Revelation Responsibly*, 16.

Another important place we find symbols in apocalyptic literature is in the use of numbers. The number seven represents completeness or perfection (thus the seven churches stand for the universal church; the seven spirits of God represent the fullness of God). The number six represents imperfection or false divinity (thus, the number of the beast is 666). Twelve can represent the fullness of God's people (the twelve tribes). Other numbers are debatable regarding their symbolic meaning (or, whether they even are symbolic). The best example here is the number one thousand and its multiples. Is it simply representative of a large (non-specific) number, or is it literal? Scholars debate back and forth on this issue.

The identification of whether a given passage in Revelation conveys an idea in symbolic or literal terms is one of the key difficulties in understanding the book, but it is not the only one. Once a reader concludes that a feature of the text is symbolic, he or she becomes obliged to ask the follow-up question: what is the reality that is symbolized?

An important principle when interpreting symbols is to remember that Revelation was written to Christians in the first century and it was understandable to them. If it had not been, nobody would have bothered to include it in the collection of inspired writings that became the New Testament. Thus, our interpretation of symbols should include consideration of how symbols could have been comprehended in the first century.

Finally, one pitfall to avoid when reading symbols in Revelation is losing the forest among the trees. Sometimes we fret so much over minutiae that we lose sight of the overall message. Revelation is designed to inspire hope and worship among the faithful and to challenge and warn the unfaithful (or, those tempted to unfaithfulness). If we focus too much on every detail, we lose sight of the message and thereby neuter Revelation of its power to speak to the church.

Alternative Perspectives

A final aspect of apocalyptic literature that we will find throughout Revelation is its ability to present readers with alternative perspectives. Historically, the people who wrote and read apocalypses tended to be those who faced adversity. Consequently, one major function of this type of writing was to say, in effect, "Things look very bad right now and will probably go on getting worse, but God is at work and will claim victory. Therefore, remain faithful in the midst of trials!"

Revelation certainly accomplished this as it spoke to the early church in the midst of persecution. In Pergamum, it appeared that the imperial cult would win as faithful people like Antipas were martyred (Rev 2:13), but Revelation opened up a heavenly vista to show that Jesus reigns and will correct what has gone wrong. He is the one who has the sharp two-edged sword (2:12) and who will one day use the sword of his mouth to speak evil into oblivion (Rev 19:15, 21).

This alternative perspective is how Revelation offers hope to the struggling people of God. It is also how it warns those who become negligent in their faith. The church is perpetually tempted to compromise by dividing its worship between the Lamb and the beast. When she makes that compromise, Revelation warns that Jesus calls for our sole allegiance and any compromise in this regard constitutes an act of unfaithfulness. When the church compromises, Jesus threatens removal of her lampstand from before God. Thus, the alternative perspective of Revelation calls us to repentance and the worship of the one true God.

6. Conclusion

We have spent a bit of time discussing the type of writing that we encounter in Revelation because understanding any type of writing depends on familiarity with its form. If I do not know how to read fantasy and instead read it as history, I will find *The Hobbit* a very confusing book. For this reason, it is important that we remember that Revelation is a hybrid of several types of writing. It is a letter written to seven churches. It is the culmination of Israel's prophetic tradition that proclaims God's words to his people. And it is an apocalypse: it is a revelation of and from Jesus that offers an alternative perspective to the church on how we are to live and conduct ourselves in this present world.

Because most modern readers find apocalyptic writing utterly foreign, we have taken extra time to explore this genre of literature. Be that as it may, this chapter has been too brief to offer an adequate introduction to apocalyptic writing. That is why, before we dive into Revelation itself, chapter two will consider another ancient Christian apocalyptic work to illustrate how apocalyptic writing operates.

In the next chapter, we study an excerpt from the Shepherd of Hermas as an entry point into apocalyptic literature. The Shepherd of Hermas was a second-century Christian book that many churches of the time believed was inspired. In fact, before the church identified the twenty-seven books of today's New Testament, the Shepherd of Hermas was taken by many Christians to have a great deal of authority, just as Revelation does.

Appendix A includes excerpts from the Shepherd of Hermas. Although chapter 2 is understandable on its own, those who read appendix A first will get more out of the material. The purpose in reading from the Shepherd of Hermas is not to add to Scripture or to advocate the importance of this writing for Christian use in worship today. Rather, the point is to acquaint us with the type of writing we find in Revelation. Just as the best way to learn a language is to immerse yourself in a culture that speaks that language, the best way to understand apocalyptic literature is to begin reading examples of apocalyptic literature.

For Further Study

Discussion Questions

1. Which type of writing contained in Revelation do you feel most comfortable reading?
2. What struggles do you think you will have in reading apocalyptic literature?
3. If we created a spectrum of different readers of Revelation ranging from those who read the Scripture very literally to very symbolically, where would you find yourself on that spectrum?

For Further Reading

- Kimberly Majeski. "Eschatology." In *Global Wesleyan Encyclopedia of Biblical Theology*, edited by Robert Branson, 117–20. Kansas City, Beacon Hill. 2020.
- Michael Gorman. "What Are We Reading? The Form of Revelation." In *Reading Revelation Responsibly: Uncivil Worship and Witness; Following the Lamb into the New Creation*, 10–30. Eugene: Cascade, 2011.

2

Eschatology and Apocalyptic Literature

Preparatory reading:

- Appendix A

1. Introduction

When I began to pastor in central Idaho, the proper identification of animals became more important for me than it had been previously. Sharing life with people in this part of the country meant I quickly found myself investing in fishing and hunting equipment, two activities that I had not practiced previously. But these new hobbies also came with challenges. Fishing required me to know the difference between bull trout and brook trout. One is okay to keep in Idaho; the other is not. Similarly, for those who hunt, it is important to distinguish mule deer from white tail deer and black bears (which can be brown in central Idaho) from grizzle bears.

Whether people are hunters, fishers, zookeepers, or nature lovers, we identify different animals by patterns and variations. The shape of a tail, the hump on a back, the coloration pattern of scales. These are clues to the identity of the animals we encounter.

In biblical studies, that same concept applies to different kinds of writing. We can understand the message and art of a psalm by comparing it to other poetic works from the ancient world. We can understand the profound theological statements made in the Bible's creation accounts by comparing—and contrasting—them to non-biblical creation stories.

By the same token, a good entry point for understanding an apocalyptic book such as Revelation is familiarize ourselves with other examples of apocalyptic writing. Doing so helps us understand that Revelation is not simply an odd book—albeit inspired—with strange symbols. Rather, it was written with a message designed to be understandable for the early church. After all, it was that church that ultimately decided to include Revelation within its list of sacred writings.

In preparation for this chapter, appendix A provided an excerpt from a second-century Christian book called the Shepherd of Hermas. As we seek to comprehend the kind of book Revelation is, Hermas will assist in our exploration of apocalyptic literature and its use of symbols.

2. Keep On Keepin' On: The Theme and Message of Hermas

Appendix A introduced us to a man named Hermas and two visions he received. In the visions, Hermas beheld symbols representing the church and those symbols were interpreted by a woman who was also a symbolic personification of the church. She explained the visions so that Hermas might understand them and convey their meaning to fellow believers of his day.

Hermas's Third Vision

The first excerpt in appendix A reports the third of five visions recorded in the Shepherd of Hermas. Prior to this vision, Hermas had fasted and prayed to receive a revelation that God had previously promised to show him. As he prayed, an old woman whom he had met in an earlier vision appeared to him and sent him into the countryside. At their meeting place, the woman showed Hermas a large square tower with men carrying different kinds of stones to it.

As Hermas and the woman spoke, she explained the symbolic nature of what Hermas saw. The tower represented the church, for which the woman was also a personification. Much of the explanation of Hermas' vision focused on the different kinds of stones used in the construction of the tower. The finest of these stones fitted perfectly together and symbolized the leaders of the church: apostles, bishops, teachers, and deacons. Other stones symbolized those who had suffered persecution for their faith in Jesus. These stones fitted in nicely with the others. A third category of stones was polished and represented believers who walked consistently in the ways of the Lord and obeyed his commandments.

There were also stones that Hermas saw cast to the side when they arrived at the tower. The woman explained these were people who had sinned and wished to repent. Upon their repentance, they would be included in the building of the tower. She further explained that time was short and the time to turn back to Christ is now, lest the building be completed and time run out.

Hermas saw several other types of stones in the vision, all of which represented different kinds of believers (or, people who had walked away from the faith). Space does not permit an analysis of each of these. What is important is that after the woman explained the stones to Hermas, the vision came to a climax with Hermas instructing his readers regarding how we should respond to the vision. His instruction was clear: the tower—the church—will soon reach completion and the time to repent has nearly elapsed. Therefore, those who enjoy living in sin must turn to Christ now to prevent exclusion from his people.

One specific group of believers Hermas addresses is the wealthy within the church. He chides them for their abundance when others experience their bodies wasting away from malnourishment. Hermas instructed the well-to-do in the church to seek out the hungry and feed them. In a statement reminiscent of Jas 5:4–5, he said if the rich fail to do this, the poor may call out to God and the rich would be shut out of the tower.

Our excerpt from Hermas's third vision concludes with an address he made to the leaders of the church. He warned them about their need for purity and unity. Apparently there had been dissensions among them. Hermas warned them about this and called those who instruct God's people also to instruct one another.

Hermas's Fourth Vision

Twenty days following Hermas's third vision he received a fourth while walking in the countryside. Before the vision, he heard a voice calling, "Doubt not, Hermas."[1] As he pondered that warning, he encountered a large and terrifying beast that resembled a sea monster in its enormity (older English translations say "whale" to help us visualize the size). It spewed

---

1. Crombie, "Pastor of Hermas," vis. 4 (ANF 2:17)

fiery locusts from its mouth, made loud noises, and had four colors on its head: black, fiery and bloody, golden, and white.

Although terrified, Hermas remembered the call not to doubt, trusted in God's salvation, and moved past the beast. The beast did not attack and Hermas discovered only later that this was due to the invisible intervention of an angel named Thegri. Once past the beast, Hermas encountered a virgin woman whom he recognized as a younger version of the same woman he saw in his previous visions; she was the church.

The woman praised Hermas for escaping the beast by trusting in God and explained that the beast represents tribulation that is coming towards God's people. They, like Hermas, must persevere in faith without doubting. If they do, they too will be delivered through the tribulation. After their conversation, the woman disappeared and the story ended abruptly with Hermas thinking the beast was returning.

3. Some Apocalyptic Observations

As we consider the apocalyptic elements of the Shepherd of Hermas, there are several points of comparison to the book of Revelation. Three observations merit our attention: (1) the use of symbols, (2) the eschatological and present importance of the work, and (3) the dual nature of the audience of the composition

Symbols

Like Revelation, the Shepherd of Hermas is filled with symbols. Some of these symbols are stock—or, routine—imagery within the apocalyptic genre. For instance, the locusts emanating from the beast seem to be a trope for apocalyptic works. In Rev 9:1–11, we find similar locusts that receive much more attention (other apocalyptic works also feature locusts).

The colors of the beast's head constitute another symbol in Hermas' fourth vision: black, red (fiery and bloody), golden, and white. Colors have significance in other apocalyptic works, as well. Colors are also significant in Revelation, such as in the story of the four horsemen (Rev 6:1–6). In both Revelation and Hermas, the colors convey meaning: Revelation's black horse ushers in famine and disaster; in Hermas, black represents the condition of the world out of which God calls his people. In both cases, the church must leave behind the disastrous spiritual condition of our world for life with Christ.

Similarly, in Revelation the color red represents violence and bloodshed (Rev 6:3–4). In Hermas, the red hues of fire and blood stand for the destruction of the world as we know it. Fire refines metals from their impurities and this leads to the golden color of the beast in Hermas. As fire burns away the dross, so those who follow God are purified by means of passing through the fire. In Hermas, the fire also gives way to the white, which represents the age to come where God's people dwell spotless and pure with him. Likewise, in Revelation white connotes cleanness and purity and describes the garb of the faithful and martyrs (Rev 3:4–5; 6:11).

It is important to understand that apocalyptic symbols often lack one-to-one correlations to the realities they represent. For instance, in Hermas's third vision, the church is symbolized in two ways simultaneously: *both* the woman speaking with Hermas *and* the tower under construction represent the church. Additionally, throughout Hermas's different visions, the woman who symbolizes the church appears to him in different forms (sometimes she is an old lady; other times she is a young woman). The point is that apocalyptic writings sometimes depict one reality in different ways. We find this in Revelation also: God's faithful people can symbolically take the form of an innumerable multitude (7:9) and as 144,000 people (7:1–8). Sometimes interpreters feel each of those entities in Rev 7 must symbolize independent groups, but consideration of how symbols operate in apocalyptic books like Hermas helps us comprehend their function in Revelation too.

As we have said, one reality can take several forms in an apocalypse. The inverse of this point is also true: one symbol can stand for multiple realities. For instance, in Rev 17:9–10, the heads of the beast stand both for seven hills and seven kings. Likewise, in Hermas' fourth vision, the one beast conveys several levels of meaning. On one level, it anticipates a coming trial that the church must endure. That trial is both eschatological (relating to the end of time), but also is present in the here and now. On another level, the beast represents the world from which believers flee (black and red colors). We are called out of the world. Nevertheless, the call out is a spiritual, not geographical call. Thus, the beast's golden color also conveys that it is in this world with its trials that the church is refined by her trust in Christ. An important point, then, is that escape from the beast includes endurance through tribulation at least as much as (if not more than) avoidance of tribulation. Revelation will make very similar points when it speaks about the trials of following Jesus.

All of this leads very quickly to another important observation about apocalyptic literature: it addresses both present realities and points to God's ultimate (eschatological) salvation and judgment.

Eschatological and Present Significance

Apocalyptic literature displays an impressive ability to speak to different time frames simultaneously. Being eschatological by definition, apocalypses speak about God's final salvation and judgment. They enlarge human history and experience to a cosmic scale and portray our struggle as a struggle between good and evil, God and the devil, etc.

As apocalypses do this, it is easy to miss that it is the reader's history they portray in this manner; it is *our* history. Books like the Shepherd of Hermas and Revelation were not recognized as important to the early church because they disclosed events that would occur centuries or millennia after their writing. They were recognized as important because they spoke—and speak—to the church of "now," whenever "now" might be. In the first and second centuries, the church faced many trials and tribulations as part of its struggle that is not against flesh and blood. Hermas and Revelation describe that struggle and continue to address the church today, which still finds herself enduring immense testing of her faithfulness to Christ.

Christians have a theological conviction that facilitates this dual focus on the present and future: the New Testament's insistence that the death and resurrection of Jesus has issued in a new age and initiated the conclusion of the present age. In other words, the era in which the church finds itself is one in which the age of the kingdom of God overlaps with the age of sin and death. Jesus alluded to this point in the Gospels when he spoke of God's kingdom as a present reality. Paul made it explicit when he explained that Jesus the Messiah "gave himself for our sins, so he could deliver us from the present evil age." (Gal 1:4, author's translation).[2] Similarly, in Rom 12:2, Paul urged the church not to conform to the patterns of this age, but to be transformed by the renewing of our mind. Christians are transformed as we live in the age to come, the age of the Messiah's resurrection.

That age has been inaugurated in the resurrection of Jesus, but it has not yet arrived in its fullness. Consequently, we also live in the present age

---

2. Author translations from the NA[28]. See Aland et al., *Novum Testamentum Graece*.

of death and destruction in which the church experiences trials and testing of her faith.

That is why apocalyptic books like Hermas and Revelation speak to two ages simultaneously. They address the church that exists as those called by God into the work of the new age Jesus inaugurated—the church that is not at home in this world. But these books also speak to the church that remains in the old world of sin. In that environment, apocalyptic books call the church to faithfulness in the present evil age and warns those who enjoy life in the present evil age to repent and answer the Messiah's call out of it and into life with him.

The Dual Audience

A final observation arising out of our exploration of the Shepherd of Hermas alongside Revelation is that both texts presuppose a readership consisting of two types of people. In addition, they are written in such a way that each group of readers will hear a different message.

On one hand, followers of Jesus receive hope in these pages even as they die for their faith through resisting the calls for allegiance issued by their governments (whether those are governments like North Korea and Iran, or the United States of America and Canada). Apocalypses remind of us the eternal perspective that God is at work and demands faithfulness to Jesus. Here, we find ourselves in the group of bloodied martyrs of Revelation who receive victory. Or, to use Hermas's imagery, we are reminded that our trials and pain hew us for inclusion within God's construction of the church.

On the other hand, both books also speak words of warning. Revelation and Hermas call to repentance those who would compromise their faithfulness. Jesus was clear in his warnings to Christians in Sardis and Laodicea (Rev 3:1–6, 14–22): if they did not reclaim their allegiance to him, he would remove their lampstands from before God. Translation: he would reject them as part of his church. When we refuse to follow Christ or seek other paths to salvation, we become the stones rejected for inclusion within the tower of the church.

4. Conclusion: A Unifying Principle for Reading Revelation

Our exploration of the Shepherd of Hermas as apocalyptic literature has offered some helpful starting points for reading Revelation. We have considered how symbols operate in this type of writing. We have also seen apocalyptic literature's ability to address the church at different points in history as it offers both hope and calls for repentance.

All of this leads to the reason many contemporary Christians never attempt to read Revelation well: *it's difficult!* It is not a simple book to understand since it is impossible to keep every important matter for interpretation in mind: how symbols work in apocalyptic literature, what was happening historically in the first century, how Revelation specifically construes an issue, etc. Holding all of this together is difficult enough, but then there are hundreds of interpreters in our time putting forth "simple" or "literal" readings of the Scripture that run in contradictory directions. How do we wade through all of that?

What makes Revelation so difficult is its readers quickly find our wheels spinning in the mud of an interpretive bog. Is there anything that can provide traction to move forward? Identifying unifying themes in any biblical book can be tricky, but in Revelation the call to faithful worship of the Lamb is front and center. Revelation is a book about worship. One of the most important passages for reading Revelation is chapter 4, which describes a perpetual worship service around the throne in heaven. This is worship directed where it should go.

The problem in Revelation is that there are many other entities that demand our worship. There are beasts and monsters and governments who would very happily own our allegiance or call us to compromise by serving them too. This is nothing other than misdirected worship and Revelation proclaims through the lure of idolatry that we must worship the Lamb alone.

As we begin to explore the book of Revelation, keep worship in mind. It is a key to understanding the book. It is also a helpful tool in evaluating the work of those who write about Revelation. If a study on Revelation does not point us to proper worship of Christ, it has most assuredly missed the point. Perhaps such studies leave us with imaginative and intriguing examples of how a prophecy may be fulfilled, but if they fail to encourage a life of faithfulness—or, if they fail to call us to be free from false worship—they may well be a false understanding of the prophetic call to worship Christ alone.

In Revelation Jesus calls to a church that lives in Babylon and says, "Come out of her, my people" (Rev 18:4). This is a call to worship and communion with him. Let those with ears to hear listen to what the Spirit says to the churches.

For Further Study

Discussion Questions

1. What was one aspect from the Shepherd of Hermas that you found encouraging?
2. Having read appendix A, can you think of any places of comparison to Revelation that were not discussed above?
3. Where can you see the theme of worship in Revelation?

3

A Revelation

Preparatory reading:

- Revelation 1
- Daniel 7:9–14
- Exodus 19:1–5

1. Introduction

When I was assigned reading materials in college, I typically followed assignment directions to the letter . . . I would not voluntarily do extra reading. As a result, I often skipped a book's introduction and went straight to chapter 1. By the time I finished graduate studies, I figured out that introductions are very helpful tools for understanding a book. Usually, the main points of the assigned reading were already articulated in the introduction, which offered a mental road map for where the writer was heading.

As with other books, the introduction to Revelation is crucial. Its opening words are foundational: "The revelation of Jesus Christ" (Rev 1:1, NASB). Two important points become apparent in this opening. First, observe that the word "revelation" is singular. English speakers often call the Bible's final book the "book of Revelations" (plural). This misunderstands the title. It is one revelation and that revelation was given to Jesus by the Father and transmitted to John through an angel (Rev 1:1). Second, John bears witness to this word from God, which he clarifies was not only given through Jesus but is also about Jesus (1:2).

Following those opening words, some of the core themes of Revelation appear. We find the theme of witnessing, as well as an initial portrait of the exalted Jesus. We also begin to glimpse an additional component of Revelation: its political nature. The claims made about Jesus are both theological and political. As a result, being a faithful witness to him and the gospel will include theological and political characteristics. In this chapter, we will survey each of these themes from Rev 1.

2. Witnessing and Martyrdom (Revelation 1:1-2)

The notion of witnessing—or, bearing testimony—arises in the second verse of Revelation and will continue as an important theme throughout the book. The Greek root translated as "witness" or "testimony" appears in various forms nearly twenty times throughout Revelation. The word for testimony (*martyria*) designates the action of one who testifies—or witnesses about something—a *martys* (martyr). In Revelation, a witness is one who testifies and holds to that testimony even to the point of death.

The content of the church's testimony is the message of Christ crucified. This is "the word of God and the testimony about Jesus" that John proclaimed (Rev 1:2, 9). In the Roman world, the very thought of worshiping a crucified God was scandalous. Ancient peoples would have deemed any deity who got himself humiliated and killed by those he came to save as either impotent or a village idiot within the pantheon, and perhaps both.

A piece of graffiti etched in the plaster of a building in Rome around 200 CE provides a representative Roman reaction to the "good news" of a crucified Jewish Messiah: the etching depicted a man with a donkey's head hanging on a cross with another man worshiping him off to the left. The inscription read, "Alexamnos worships his god." This picture, while insulting, is the earliest depiction of Jesus' crucifixion historians have recovered.[1]

The Christians' willingness to cling to the testimony about a crucified Jesus who is also Lord and God made little sense to Romans and created a major rift between Christians and society at large. That society accepted Caesar as the lord to be worshiped and for whom grand temples were erected. Especially in Asia Minor, emperor worship constituted a significant part

---

1. To view the picture, see Chapman, "Crucifixion in Paul."

of civil life and most people would have found the idea of worshiping a crucified Messiah incomprehensible.

Revelation counters that societal perception by giving an alternate apocalyptic perspective of what transpires behind the scenes. While humiliating, the crucifixion was also God's victory in achieving salvation for the world. This is why Jesus, the slaughtered lamb of Rev 5, can take the scroll from God's hand and unseal his plan of salvation and judgment. The shame of apparent defeat in crucifixion was also the victory of God. We experience that victory graphically in the revelation the Father gave Jesus to show his servants (Rev 1:1).

That revelation is the testimony about Jesus and his lordship and it is the witness proclaimed by the church. Through stubborn commitment to this proclamation, the church would conquer, not with swords, but by becoming witnesses to what God has accomplished. That is the victory Revelation depicts when it speaks about Christians overcoming the beast by the word of their testimony. Like Jesus' victory, the church's triumph would appear to be a defeat, but the heavenly perspective of the apocalypse reveals that the martyr's (witness's) death leads to vindication and eternal life.

3. The Politics of Theology (Revelation 1:4–8)

Its depiction of the spiritual conflict between the church and society is one of the chief contributions Revelation makes to New Testament theology. In a world that confessed Caesar as lord, Revelation insisted that Jesus is "the faithful witness, the firstborn of the dead, and the ruler of the kings of the earth" (Rev 1:5).

While such descriptions of Jesus become routine for twenty-first century Christians in the Western hemisphere, the notions that Jesus rules the kings of the earth (Rev 1:5), that he established a kingdom made of his followers (1:9), and that he formed his followers into a kingdom of priests (1:6) were treasonous in ancient Rome. Such confessions meant that Caesar could not be lord in any meaningful sense of the word; his rule was subjugated under the true lordship of Jesus. Consequently, the citizens of Jesus' kingdom found themselves (as they still do today) on a collision course with the kingdoms of this world.

Revelation nests profound political claims within its theological outlook. Jesus is not simply the latest in a long line of human rulers. His right to rule is bound up in his identity as the resurrected one, the firstborn from the dead, whose name God highly exalted so that every tongue will confess, "Jesus is Lord" (Phil 2:9–11). Significantly, as ruler, Jesus is also the one who loves us and freed us from our sins by his blood (Rev 1:5).

Revelation 1 holds in tandem the humiliation and the exaltation of Jesus. In his blood, we find the crucified one who died in shame. In the resurrection, we find the glorified one who rules creation. We see that glorified portrait in Rev 1, which offers such an exalted glimpse of Christ that it introduces another important theological contribution made by Revelation: Jesus' divinity.

Jews did not necessarily anticipate that the Messiah would be divine and it took Christians several centuries to articulate the mystery of Jesus' full divinity and full humanity. Even so, Revelation makes an important contribution to our understanding of Christ's nature by describing Jesus in ways similar to the Father. Jesus' self-description echoes that of the Father. Whereas the Father in Rev 1:8 and 21:5–6 said, "I am the Alpha and the Omega" (the first and last letters of the Greek alphabet), Jesus also identified himself in this way in 22:13 (cf. Rev 1:17). By applying similar titles both to Jesus and the Father, Revelation bolsters the church's belief that Jesus is God. We also glimpse the divinity of Jesus when we recognize that Revelation insists God alone is to be worshiped even as it depicts creation worshiping Jesus (Rev 5:13–14). Likewise, it is significant that the Lamb does not occupy his own throne, but resides on God's throne (Rev 7:17; 22:1).

This picture of the glorified Jesus is remarkable and we can hardly imagine the impact it would have had to John's first readers. Those from Jewish backgrounds would have found themselves rethinking their conception of monotheism—the belief in one God. If Jesus is divine, how does he relate to God in the Old Testament and how can we retain the belief in only one God? This would have been the question of John's Jewish readers. His non-Jewish readers likewise would experience difficulty. The imperial cult was prevalent in the region where Revelation first circulated. The claim to Jesus' divinity and lordship was in direct competition with the politico-religious claims of the empire.

4. A Picture of Jesus (Revelation 1:9–17)

John began his story about an encounter with Jesus by describing what he heard: a sound like a trumpet told him to write what he would see and to send it to the seven churches (Rev 1:9–11).

When he turned around, John beheld a truly awe-inspiring vision of Jesus. In the midst of seven lampstands stood one like a son of man in a robe reaching to his feet. Across his chest was a golden sash, his hair was white like wool and snow, and he eyes were fiery. If that picture is not awesome enough, John continues: his feet were like bronze glowing from the heat of a furnace and his voice roared like many waters. He held seven stars in his hand, from his mouth came a double-edged sword, and his face shined with all the brilliance of the sun.

In a world that lacked anything like Hollywood's cinematic photography and special effects, this description of Jesus would spark the imagination. People who heard Rev 1 read aloud would visualize one whose face was as bright and blinding as the sun, whose feet glowed like molten metal, and who possessed in one hand the stars that hang so far out of reach for any of us. Hearing this description of Jesus in places like Pergamum would enlist a person's imagination in service to an exalted theology proclaiming Christ's divinity.

In addition to its use of visual effects, Revelation fires our imaginations through its use of the Old Testament. Throughout our investigation of Rev 1–22, we will see the book routinely drawing upon and refashioning the Old Testament. In Rev 1:12–20, the portrait of Jesus employs imagery reminiscent of Dan 7. In Daniel, the prophet reported a vision of the Ancient of Days who gave authority and dominion to one called a "Son of Man" (Dan 7:9–28). The imagery of both figures appears in Revelation 1:12–20. Like the second figure in Dan 7, Jesus is called a "son of man" (Rev 1:13). Likewise, both individuals receive an eternal dominion (Dan 7:14; Rev 1:6, 18).

Through using this imagery, Rev 1 equates Daniel's Son of Man with Jesus. But Revelation also goes farther than this by depicting Jesus in ways that resemble Daniel's Ancient of Days, who sat on a throne with clothing white as snow and woolly white hair. John modifies this in Rev 1:13–16. No longer is he concerned with the color of the robe, but the whiteness of Jesus' hair resembles both wool and snow. Similarly, the flame of Jesus' eyes and his glowing feet (Rev 1:14–15) vaguely echo the blazing flames of the throne in Daniel 7:9.

New Testament scholar N. T. Wright has summarized well John's reason for associating Jesus with both Daniel's Son of Man and the Ancient of Days: "In John's vision, these two pictures seem to have merged. When we are looking at Jesus, he is saying, we are looking straight through him at the father himself."² To use Jesus' own words: "The one who has seen Me has seen the Father" (John 14:9).

This glorified portrait of Jesus has significant implications for the lived experience of Christians today. The Jesus that we encounter is indeed the friend of sinners. He is the loving shepherd who seeks out lost sheep. Even so, we must hold the immanence of Jesus in tension with his transcendence. The closeness and intimacy of Jesus is best appreciated when we realize that this one who enters in to dine with us is also the lord of all creation. He is one with the Ancient of Days and holds authority not only over the kingdoms of our world but over the personified evils of Death and Hades as well (Rev 1:19).

This Jesus boggles our imaginations. Imagine standing next to one whose face shined like the sun. Imagine hearing the deafening sound of a massive waterfall and then recognizing the voice of Jesus echoing through that roar. When we put ourselves in John's shoes, we recognize his response was completely natural: he fell on his face is fear and awe. Then, this same Jesus touched John and spoke with his roaring, yet soothing, voice: "Don't be afraid."³ What a privilege it is to speak with this person and to commune with him in prayer! What a responsibility it is to serve him and—to use Paul's language—to unite as his body!

Another way John kindles the reader's imagination is through his use of political imagery. Jesus' depiction as one grasping seven stars is an example of this (Rev 1:16). During emperor Domitian's reign (81–96 CE), Rome minted a gold coin depicting a young boy playing with seven stars while sitting atop a globe. The coin commemorated the emperor's recently deceased son whom he declared divine and depicted as the god Jupiter on the coin. In the ancient world, there were seven astral bodies that people considered divine: the sun, moon, and five planets visible without the assistance of telescopes (Mercury, Venus, Mars, Jupiter, and Saturn). To depict the child playing with these figures while sitting astride a globe was both a theological and political claim made by Domitian.

In Revelation, Jesus co-opts that message. He is not an emperor's dead son, but the Living One who is King of the rulers of the earth. From his mouth comes the sharp two-edged sword whose words spoke creation into existence in Gen 1 and who will speak evil into nonexistence in Rev 19:15 (see Rev 19:21). This Jesus holds the seven luminaries in his hand, but they

---

2. Wright, *Revelation for Everyone*, 8.
3. Wright, *Revelation for Everyone*, 8.

are no longer deified parts of creation. Rather, they represent the angels who stand as the heavenly counterparts of the churches to whom Revelation is addressed (Rev 1:20).

Those churches, as has been noted, were seven in number. The number seven is both literal and symbolic. Revelation was written to churches in seven different cities. However, as the number of completion, or perfection, the seven also stand as a mosaic picture of the universal church. Thus, Revelation speaks not only to Christians in Philippi and Smyrna; it also speaks to the church throughout history and around the globe. It is to the description of this church that we must turn next.

5. Conclusion: The Church's Life Between Jesus and Caesar

The church of Revelation consists of the people who faithfully bear witness to the true identity of Jesus as "the firstborn of the dead, and the ruler of the kings of the earth" (Rev 1:5). It is the people who insist that, despite all appearances, Jesus is Lord. Many of these people would suffer and die for their proclamation of this message; they would become martyrs.

The reason the stakes are so high as life and death has nothing to do with the apocalyptic message of Revelation speaking about some phantasmal heavenly throne room. Rather, they are high because the theological message touches our world; it has political ramifications. Confessing Jesus as Lord impacts for how one lives on earth. If Jesus is Lord in any meaningful sense of the term, then Caesar is not.

The struggle for the church today is that the Caesars of the twenty-first century respond to their dethronement by Jesus just about as well as the imperial cult did in John's time. Caesars have no interest in surrendering the throne. In this, we are not necessarily speaking about a monarchy or dictatorship. Caesars can also be elected. Caesar is whatever cries out for the loyalty of those in the church. It is whatever and whoever—besides Jesus—says "follow me."

Caesar is greater than any one person. He demands our allegiance and worship while masking himself in all sorts of ways. Sometimes worship of Caesar comes in the form of patriotic and nationalistic attempts to syncretize with Christian worship. Such attempts divert our attention away from the Lamb an onto something else (a political position, a flag, a holiday, etc.). Sometimes this takes the form of important social issues and tells us to give ourselves to one or another cause when that cause interestingly seems to put the same people in power who have been in office for decades.

Caesar comes in all shapes and sizes and seldom identifies himself as such, but the church recognizes him by his fruit when she refuses to surrender her allegiance. When the church refuses to worship Caesar, when she resists the temptation to take up arms in whatever the social crisis *du jour* might be, when she willingly surrenders her freedoms to serve Christ, Caesar becomes irate. The church attracts his ire because its surrender to Christ proclaims that Jesus owns the church's allegiance and Caesar does not. That is a situation Caesar cannot tolerate because it dissolves the illusions of his sovereignty, permanence, and divinity. When the Christian faith removes such deceptions, opposition comes quickly from the deceivers. It is precisely this kind of a faith and testimony that landed John in exile on the island of Patmos, thirty-five miles off the coast of southwest Turkey. The faithful church very quickly becomes the persecuted church.

Revelation is written to that people—as well as those who have colluded with Caesar—to provide the heavenly perspective that as Caesar rages on, Jesus is the Living One who holds the keys to Death and Hades. The worst Caesar can do is kill Christians for their proclamation, but Jesus has victory over death. He is forming his people into a kingdom of priests, which is what he has been doing ever since God met Israel at Mount Sinai (Exod 19:6). As that people, the church's role in the trials of her age is to witness faithfully to Jesus' true identity as King. This is a task for which she requires encouragement and instruction and that is exactly what Jesus offers her in Rev 2–3.

For Further Study

Discussion Questions

1. Imagine yourself as John deep in prayer on Patmos when he was confronted by the amazing imagery of Rev 1:12–16. What do you imagine you would have felt or perceived in that experience?
2. Identify three places where the confession of Jesus as Lord might challenge something that calls for your allegiance politically.
3. In what ways does witnessing in Revelation differ from how Evangelical Americans typically employ the term?

4

Letters to the Churches

Preparatory reading:

- Revelation 2–3

1. Introduction

For many of us, letters are a thing of the past. Most of our important communications today occur through other means: the internet, cell phones, emails, etc. The majority of the letters I receive fall into one of two categories: *bills* or *junk*. I was much more excited as a child when I found something in the mailbox with my name on it. I would often receive letters from my grandfather on the other side of the country and wanted to hear what was happening in his life. It was a big deal!

Letters were big deals in the ancient world too. This was before printing, ballpoint pens, and factory produced paper. Letters were written on a mesh of papyrus and inscribed with ink that required its own process to produce. Writing was not cheap. As such, most people seldom received such a gift. With that in mind, imagine the excitement of Christians in a house church in Thyatira when they received a letter from their exiled pastor, John. Then, imagine the thrill they must have experienced as he reported his vision of Jesus and enclosed letters *to them* from Jesus.

For its first audiences, Revelation was a thrill to receive and to hear read aloud. But it also conveyed challenging words. Jesus began his message to each of the seven churches with the words "I know . . ." For some of the churches, Jesus' knowledge was comforting: *he knows our struggles and is encouraging us*. For other churches, Jesus' knowledge of their works highlighted the need for repentance: *he knows that we have been unfaithful*.

The letters to the churches in Rev 2–3 provide a key for reading the rest of the book. Whether one hears hope or threats in Revelation depends on which church one attends. If you are part of a faithful community, Revelation is cause for rejoicing because the Lamb is on the throne. However, if you find yourself in a church of divided allegiances, the message of Revelation is a call to repentance so that you might return to faithful worship of God.

In this chapter, we will explore the background of each of Jesus' letters to the seven churches before pausing to reflect on the connection between religion and everyday civil life in the Roman world. Following that, the challenge will be for us to consider where we find ourselves within the spectrum of the churches that first read Revelation.

2. Ephesus (Revelation 2:1–7)

Ephesus was arguably the most important city in the region. Culturally, it boasted a proud Greek heritage and was home to the temple of Artemis, one of the seven wonders of the ancient world. Though it is now landlocked, in the first-century Ephesus was an important port city that was also situated along a major road, which provided a strong economy.

Prior to Revelation, Paul had an effective ministry in Ephesus (Acts 19). Indeed, he was so effective that the silversmith industry incited a riot over its economic losses claiming that the temple of Artemis would fall into disgrace. That concern hit a cultural pressure point and enflamed a people who were passionate about their history and took pride in their magnificent temple.

Years later, in Rev 2, Jesus praised the Ephesian church for its perseverance and endurance. As with each of the seven letters, this one begins by noting the recipient: the angel of the church in Ephesus. In Rev 2–3, the angels of the churches are angelic personifications of the seven churches. Thus, by addressing the angel, Jesus addressed the church. Along with the recipient, Jesus also included an introductory statement reminiscent of the Old Testament prophets: "Thus says the one who holds the seven stars in his right hand and who walks among the seven gold lampstands . . ." (2:1, author's translation).

This introduction accomplishes two feats. First, it identifies the message to follow as a prophetic utterance. Just as prophets like Isaiah and Jeremiah stood before God's people saying, "Thus says the Lord," now the Lord himself utters the prophetic oracle to the church through the prophet-pastor, John.

Secondly, Jesus' description of himself employs imagery already seen in Rev 1. Any prophetic message from the individual John saw in Rev 1 is no message to disregard. The church that faced pressure to worship Artemis and the emperor now received a letter from its true sovereign: the one who walks among the seven golden lampstands representing the church and who holds the stars (representing the angels of the churches) in his right hand (see 1:16). Jesus does not speak as the humble, foot-washing servant of John 13. Now he addresses his followers as Lord.

The Ephesian church was neither fully faithful nor completely unfaithful. Like most churches, it was a mixture. Jesus praised its perseverance and endurance. Amid economic and cultural pressures to participate in the cult of Artemis, Ephesian Christians had not grown weary in their refusal to deny Jesus' name (2:3). Furthermore, they were zealous for orthodoxy. Perhaps because they lived in a place where the cultural current pushed strongly toward the worship of Artemis, the Christians in Ephesus were diligent to test false apostles (Rev 2:2) and to reject them along with people who adhered to heresies like that of the Nicolaitans (2:6).

Nevertheless, there was also a problem: in its zeal for orthodoxy, the church had forgotten its first love. The problem was not the Ephesian concern for correct belief. Rather, it was a disconnect between belief and action. Correct belief points the church toward faithful love and worship of Jesus and to the love of our neighbors. When we lose our love of Jesus, when we neglect to love our neighbors by serving them and showing hospitality, we have failed with respect to the greatest commandments that Scripture gives us. This is why Jesus threatened to remove the church's lampstand (2:5)

In addition to repentance, Jesus called his people to remember from where they had fallen (Rev 2:5). Remembering what God has done in the life of the church is a remedy for spiritual dryness. As we recall the Holy Spirit's presence and loving activity on our behalf, we cannot help but yearn for the passion we once possessed. This will lead us to repentance by doing the works we had done at first: works of worship and of loving service to him and our neighbors.

In true apocalyptic form, Jesus' letter to the church in Ephesus offers an alternate perspective on reality. He reminds us that there is more to following him than zealous orthodoxy. Zealous love is paramount. With repentance and faithfulness, the church will become victorious. Jesus promises to grant those who overcome access to the tree of life (cf. Gen 3). That tree appears in the new creation in Rev 22:2 and those who are found worthy of living in the New Jerusalem will enjoy its fruit.

3. Smyrna (Revelation 2:8–11)

Approximately thirty-five miles north of Ephesus sat another prosperous port city known for its early and consistent loyalty to Rome—Smyrna. In 195 BCE, the city constructed a temple to Roma, the goddess of Rome. Subsequently, the Roman senate rewarded Smyrna's loyalty with permission to construct a temple dedicated to Emperor Tiberius in 26 CE. In John's time, Smyrna remained a thriving center for the imperial cult.

In that cultural environment, the populace considered anyone who refused to sacrifice to the emperor to be unpatriotic and unreligious. Such claims created economic hardships (e.g., loss of customers at one's business) as well as persecution. But there was one group in Smyrna that could avoid successfully many of the pressures of emperor worship: the Jews, who had reached an agreement with Rome that exempted them from emperor worship. Christians enjoyed these privileges too, as long as they were considered a Jewish sect, which was exactly how Roman officials perceived Christians: they followed a Jewish Messiah, worshiped the Jewish deity, and read the Jewish Scriptures.

That is important for understanding Jesus' letter to the Smyrnean Christians. As the church grew, disagreements arose with the sizable Jewish community of Smyrna that rejected the crucified Jesus as Israel's Messiah and harbinger of God's Kingdom. Once the synagogue alerted the local officials that the Jesus-followers stood apart from Judaism, Christians became subject to several forms of persecution.

For John and his readers, this raised a question regarding who the true Israel might be. For them, as for Paul (Rom 2:25–29), true Israel was the group of people who were faithful to the Messiah. By his grace, God allowed non-Jews to become part of this people (Rom 11:11–23) so the church is not a replacement for God's promises to Israel. Be that as it may, the Israel that received God's promises was an Israel that was faithful to the covenant that pointed to the Messiah. Rejection of the Christ (the Greek word for Messiah), is a rejection of God's covenant.

In John's thinking, Jewish participation in the oppression of those worshiping the Messiah gave evidence of satanic influence. That is why he identified the synagogue as a "synagogue of Satan" and its congregants as "so-called Jews." The problem was not that God had rejected Israel; rather, it was that much of Israel rejected God and the Messiah in its attempt to squelch the worship of Jesus' followers.

Despite the fierce opposition the Christians of Smyrna faced, Jesus' letter demonstrates they did not succumb to the pressures of compromise. Jesus identified himself as "the first and the last, who was dead, but lives!" (Rev 2:8, author's translation). The crucified Messiah was also the Living One and he knew the tribulation and poverty of the Smyrnean Christians.

As with Ephesus, Jesus' letter to Smyrna provided an alternate perspective. Whereas the Christians of Smyrna were economically poor and suffered persecution, the truth of the matter was that they were spiritually rich (2:9). They had been faithful and, as such, were one of only two churches in Revelation about which Jesus had nothing negative to say. Their task was to endure through the hard times that would become even more difficult.

Jesus warned of a coming tribulation that would last ten days. This likely anticipates a local persecution of Christians which may or may not have lasted a literal ten days. As we saw in the Shepherd of Hermas, apocalyptic literature uses symbolism heavily and a round number like ten could well symbolize a time of limited duration for the persecution. Whatever the case, Smyrna did indeed experience tribulation in its ensuing history. In 156 CE, its bishop—Polycarp—would be martyred in the city.

Jesus promised that the church's faithfulness would result in a crown of life and those who were victorious through faithfulness would escape the second death (Rev 2:11), foreshadowing the punishment of those thrown into the lake of fire (see 20:14–15). Likewise the crown received by the faithful anticipates the heavenly worship service in which the twenty-four elders around the throne cast down their crowns in worship of God (4:10).

4. Pergamum (Revelation 2:12–17)

From Smyrna, Revelation travels forty-five miles northward to the provincial capital, Pergamum. The city also served as the provincial center for the imperial cult and boasted several other forms of local religion.

Its acropolis—the imposing hill that overlooks the city—housed several temples along with a massive altar dedicated to Zeus surrounded by a colonnade.

Jesus identified himself to the Pergamene Christians as the one who holds a sharp two-edged sword. He also knows where they live: they inhabit the place where Satan has his throne, which is likely a reference either to the imperial cult or to Zeus's colossal altar in Pergamum. In the first century BCE, Pergamum had erected a temple for Caesar Augustus and Roma, the deified personification of Rome.[1] Such temples afforded the city honor and recognition. Alternatively, Satan's throne may refer to the seat of the provincial governor, which was also located in the city. Perhaps each of the institutions above was in view. Whatever the case, the point remains that Pergamene Christians lived in a precarious situation. They had already witnessed the martyrdom of a believer named Antipas. He died as a faithful and true witness about Jesus and is the only named martyr in the seven letters. Despite such fierce opposition, the church of Pergamum remained faithful to Jesus.

Even so, Jesus spotlighted some troubling issues in the church, especially regarding false teachings. Some Pergamene Christians followed the "teaching of Balaam" (Rev 2:14). In the Old Testament, Balaam was a prophet hired by the king of the Amorites to curse the Israelites (Num 22:1–6). At first, Balaam appeared faithful because he obeyed when God prohibited him from cursing Israel. However, Balaam also found a more covert method of bringing a curse. Although he could not mount a direct spiritual assault, he accomplished the same effect indirectly by luring Israel into idolatry. As today, sex offered a particularly efficient way to facilitate sin. Under Balaam's advice, Midianite women began to intermarry with Israel (Num 31:16). As Israel intermarried with Midianites (and Moabites), they also began to worship their gods. Balaam's mission was now accomplished.

Like Israel, Pergamene Christians experienced the lure of idolatry. In the regional capital, civic life included worshiping the emperor and making sacrifices. Any refusal made one stick out like a sore thumb. The questions for the church were "How far is too far? Must we all be like Antipas, or can we assimilate with our culture just enough to fly under the radar? Is it okay to attend the feasts? Can we join the trade guilds that worship patron deities? Is purchasing meat at public markets attached to temples a participation in that temple's business and worship?"

---

1. DeSilva, *Discovering Revelation*, 40.

Some Christians in Pergamum believed such activities were permissible. Surely, the idolatrous words said about Caesar were meaningless for some Christians. They only went through the motions of emperor-worship and spoke about Caesar as lord in order to avoid trials and to live in peace as they worshipped Christ. Jesus' letter to Pergamum uncovers the problem with this approach: such blending with culture betrays the church's allegiance to Jesus alone. This is why Jesus took a strong position: eating meat sacrificed to idols—i.e., the meat available at public markets in Pergamum—and going with the flow is idolatry.

One group that may have gone this route was the Nicolaitans. Throughout the history of Revelation's interpretation, several speculations have emerged about this group's teaching (which is also mentioned in Rev 2:6). John gives minimal information about what the Nicolaitans believed. Consequently, most proposals tell us less about the Nicolaitans and more about those making the proposals.

More important than understanding heresy is what Jesus commands. In this case, Jesus, the one who possessed the sharp two-edged sword, warned the Christians of Pergamum to repent and adopt a lifestyle of uncompromising allegiance to him. If they failed, he would come and make war against them with the sword of his mouth (Rev 2:16). This is the same sword that Jesus wields in Rev 19:15, 21 when he strikes down those allied with the beast and his army. Failure to heed Jesus' warning would place Christians under that same sword because their idolatry bespeaks allegiance to the beast.

Conversely, if Christians in Pergamum repented, if they refused to participate in the civic and religious culture of their world, then Jesus promised to provide for them. As they abstained from meat sacrificed to idols, Jesus would provide the hidden manna, the bread God sent to sustain his people in the wilderness (Rev 2:17; see Exod 16:15). This is the alternative apocalyptic perspective offered by Revelation. Whereas the culture was starving Christians spiritually (if not physically), Jesus promised to sustain his people. He would provide a feast as they remained faithful to him and he would give them a white stone with a new name (Rev 2:17).

In Pergamum, people used white stones as admission tickets to important events such as banquets. If that comparison holds, the stone in Revelation 2:17 may be a way of saying those who are faithful—even when tempted to compromise—will receive their admission ticket into the wedding supper of the Lamb (Rev 19:7–9). Christ will feed them even as they endure physical poverty in a spiritually impoverished world.

5. Thyatira (Revelation 2:18–29)

Situated forty miles east and a little south of Pergamum sat Thyatira, known for its textile industry. In addition to textiles, the city was a hub for trade guilds that included industries related to metallurgy: work with copper, bronze, iron, as well as the creation of armor.

That background makes the description of Jesus in the letter all the more impactful. To a people familiar with metal work, Jesus called himself the son of God whose eyes are like flames of fire and whose feet are like "fine brass."[2] As with each church, Jesus knows the deeds done in Thyatira: they were faithful and righteous and had endured. Even more, their journey had an upward trajectory: recent works showed marked improvement from where they began.

Nevertheless, some wanted to compromise. Accommodation with the culture was likely part of the teachings promulgated by the prophetess Jezebel. The culture surrounding the church of Thyatira exerted pressures into religious practices that ran contrary to confessing Jesus as the one true Lord. Even in the trade guilds, one encountered religious practices that should make Christians uneasy.

Like the allusion to Balaam above, the cryptic moniker Jezebel points us to the Old Testament. She was the notorious wife of King Ahab, as well as a driving force behind the institutionalization Baal and Asherah worship in Israel (1 Kgs 18:19; see also 1 Kgs 16:31–33). As a Sidonian princess, Baal and Asherah were Jezebel's national deities and they came with her when she married King Ahab. First Kings mentions in almost one breath that Ahab married Jezebel and then went off to serve Baal.

Likewise, in Thyatira, a prominent teacher led many astray into "sexual immorality" and idolatry. It seems unlikely that sexual immorality in Rev 2:20 refers to literal sexual relations. The language recalls that of Hosea, which symbolizes idolatry as prostitution, or spiritual adultery. In both Hosea and Rev 2:18–29, God's people were "hooking up" with other gods—that is the immorality of Jezebel.

The slippery slope into idolatry created by keeping one foot in step with culture and one foot in the church is precisely why Revelation took a

---

2. An alternate translation for the NASB's "burnished bronze."

strong stance against teachings that permitted dual commitments. If a person began eating in the temple—as some Christians in Thyatira undoubtedly did—it becomes difficult to determine which other practices there might be permissible. This difficulty increases exponentially when a teacher in the church distorts the doctrine of Christian freedom to suggest morality is inconsequential. The New Testament addresses such teachings elsewhere and Jezebel may have espoused something similar to these (cf. Rom 6:1–7). Consequently, Jesus called Christians in Thyatira to avoid idolatry in any form. In all probability that avoidance included participation in the trade guilds, each of which honored a patron deity. Paying homage to anyone but Jesus is unacceptable for his followers.

Despite the problems in Thyatira, Jesus also extended patience and mercy. He warned the prophetess and granted her time to repent (2:21). The problem was she remained unwilling to repent from her (spiritual) immorality. Once people compromise their faith by getting into bed with the gods of this world (whether with Artemis and Aphrodite, the goddesses of sex and fertility; Ares, the god of war; or any other deity), it becomes horribly unpleasant to leave their embrace. That is why Jesus warned those who would commit adultery with the accommodating Jezebel: their inheritance for blending in with culture will not be luxury, but great trials and distress. Ultimately, refusal to repent will lead to death (Rev 2:22–23).

Again, Revelation offers an alternate perspective on the world the church inhabits. Whereas leaders like Jezebel teach accommodation to an idolatrous culture allows a prosperous and comfortable life, Jesus reminds his followers that straddling the fence leads to death. Conversely, the struggles of life we encounter on the narrow road of faithfulness lead to ultimate victory.

Because of its difficult situation, Jesus laid no additional challenge upon the Thyatiran Christians (2:24). Their task was to continue to avoid the teachings of Satan and to endure until Jesus returns. Jesus promised to reward such faithfulness by granting his people authority to rule over the nations, as well as giving them the bright morning star, which could symbolize a couple of things. On the one hand, the star might refer to Venus (the brightest "star" in the night sky), which symbolized authority. This would be another way of restating Jesus' promise of empowering his faithful people. On the other hand, Jesus himself is identified in Revelation as the "bright morning star" (22:16). If this allusion holds, the faithful in the church would enjoy communion with Christ in addition to receiving authority.

6. Sardis (Revelation 3:1-6)

Thirty miles south of Thyatira sat the city of Sardis adjacent to white marble cliffs. With gold deposits in the area, it had a reputation for wealth. Christians in Sardis also had a reputation: they were the thriving and vibrant church. Jesus addressed them as the one who possessed the seven spirits (representing the fullness of God's Spirit). With such divine authority, he upbraided the church for a gap between its reputation and reality: "You have a reputation of being alive, but you are dead" (3:1 NIV).

The lack of details obscures the nature of the problem, but the reference to soiled garments implies they had bent under pressure. These Christians had syncretized with society by splitting their loyalties between God and their culture. Such compromise permitted the church to flourish in terms of prosperity. But such comfort had a high price: spiritual death.

Despite appearances, Jesus deemed the works of these Christians incomplete. Outwardly, they appeared successful, but they were not fully with Jesus and this had become a critical problem. "It's all or nothing: either Jesus really is Lord, rightly asking for our absolute allegiance, or he is a sham and should be rejected outright. It simply won't do to bumble on, looking busy but achieving little or nothing. Reputation isn't enough."[3] Christians living off their reputation end up soiling their garments when they choose that reputation over faithfulness to Christ.

Jesus commanded the believers in Sardis who retained any vital signs of faithfulness to awake from their spiritual comas and repent. As in other NT passages, Jesus compared himself to a thief who would take them unawares (cf. Rev 16:15; Matt 24:43). His metaphor communicated well to the city's citizens who corporately remembered earlier times when the people trusted Sardis's reputation as an impregnable city (because of its defendable geography). However, that reputation had failed to prevent Cyrus from conquering Sardis in 546 BCE; reputation was no substitute for preparedness.

The shocking implication of Jesus' thief metaphor is that the church—not only the world—will be caught off guard when he returns. The alternate apocalyptic perspective of this letter holds up the Christians of Sardis as a reminder to Christians throughout history that spiritual life cannot be measured in terms of affluence, attendance, social action, or any other external rubric. It is measured by faithfulness to Christ and a willingness to

---

3. Wright, *Revelation for Everyone*, 30.

live and act in accordance with the confession that Jesus is Lord. Those who remain faithful will receive white and unsullied garments and will find their names written in the Book of Life (Rev 3:5; cf. 20:12, 15; 21:27).

7. Philadelphia (Revelation 3:7–13)

Nearly thirty miles south and east from Sardis sat Philadelphia—the second church to which Jesus issued no warnings; the other church was Smyrna. Also like the believers in Smyrna, the Philadelphian Christians faced political and social opposition from the Jewish community. It is easy to miss the power differential between the two groups. Philadelphia likely had a Jewish population of two to three thousand that also owned its own buildings. By contrast, the Christian (or Jewish-Christian) community was likely small and meeting in a house church.

This is important to remember when Revelation chastises "so-called Jews" in the "synagogue of Satan" (Rev 3:9). As in Smyrna, Jews and Jewish-Christians in Philadelphia were asking the question "who are the true Jews?" Those in the synagogue rejected the claims of Jesus and likely excommunicated those following him. In essence, the door into God's people—Israel—was closed for anyone claiming Jesus was the crucified and resurrected Messiah.

In the letter to Philadelphian Christians, Jesus reverses the script and declares that those refusing to acknowledge him as the Messiah are false Jews. His identity as the "one who is holy and true" legitimates Jesus' authority to make such pronouncements (Rev 3:7). Jesus' authority also appears in his possession of the keys of to the kingdom (3:7; cf. Isa 22:22). With these keys, he opens the door of the kingdom for those who follow him and no one can close it.

To the faithful Christians of Philadelphia, Jesus promised exemption from the hour of testing. Apocalyptic writings routinely described the trials of eschatological judgments (see our discussion of Hermas's fourth vision in chapter 2). Whatever the testing in Rev 3:10 might be, it is unlikely that Jesus promised the church an escape from life on earth. Remember, part of the hope extended to the Philadelphians was that their current oppressors would one day come and bow before them, presumably on earth (Rev 3:9).

For the Philadelphian Christians, the alternate perspective that Revelation presents to Jesus' followers was that despite their fragile existence under oppression, Jesus knows their faithfulness and endurance and he has promised to make them an unmovable pillar in God's temple and to inscribe his name on them.

8. Laodicea (Revelation 3:14–22)

Forty-five miles southeast of Philadelphia (or, ninety-five miles east of our starting point in Ephesus) was the town of Laodicea. Among the seven letters, this one is probably best known in North America. It includes the memorable depiction of Jesus knocking on the door, as well as the colorful imagery of him spewing the lukewarm church out of his mouth.

The lukewarm imagery was especially meaningful for Laodiceans. Eleven miles southeast was Colossae with its cool refreshing water flowing down from Mount Cadmus. That water was pure and excellent for human consumption. Also in the vicinity was Hierapolis, six miles north of Laodicea. To this day, tourists visit its famous hot springs. The problem for Laodicea was, despite its great prosperity in other areas (banking, textiles, medicine, etc.), by the time water flowed downstream to Laodicea, whether from Colossae or Hierapolis, it was lukewarm and barely drinkable. It had the effect on people that the church had on Jesus.

The Laodicean Christians suffered from spiritual indifference. Jesus would prefer them to be cool and refreshing or hot and zesty with the Spirit. Instead, they were neither. They believed they were self-sufficient and boasted of their prosperity, "*I am rich . . . I need nothing*" (Rev 3:17). The comfort of sufficiency quickly breeds complacency: if I am so at ease that I need nothing, I am less likely to recognize my need of Jesus and I certainly won't be very excited about his call to self-sacrifice.

The church of Laodicea appeared sufficient, but Jesus confronted it with an alternate apocalyptic perspective: their apparent self-sufficiency blinded them to their true spiritual condition—they were wretched and poor. They needed to use what resources they had to purchase refined gold from Jesus. Whereas Laodicea was famous for its black wool, Jesus called the church to acquire from him white garments of purity and faithfulness to cover their spiritual nakedness. They did not need the popular eye ointments available in Laodicea, but a salve that would cure spiritual blindness.

Like their cohorts in Sardis, the Laodicean Christians needed to move from the complacency of self-sufficiency to a recognition of their true need of Jesus, whom they recognized as Lord. If they would choose to move from complacency to zealous faithfulness through repentance, then Jesus—who knocks at their door—promised to come and dine with them. By overcoming in this fashion, they would sit with him on his throne.

9. Religion and the Letters of Revelation

Many North American Christians take for granted the belief that there can (or should) be a separation between religion and government. For citizens of the United States, this conviction is enshrined in the first amendment to their constitution and there is almost no quicker way to raise American hackles than to threaten the separation of church and state.

For first-century believers, that separation was unimaginable. Religion was very much a state affair, especially in Asia Minor where the imperial cult flourished. David deSilva correctly observed that such flourishing of emperor-worship was not so much imposed by Rome as it was "enthusiastically promoted at the level of the local elites."[4] Participation in religious festivals, the building of temples, and worship of the emperor became a matter of civic duty and pride, thereby forging the connection between politics and religion under examination in Revelation.

Revelation's theology becomes political by affirming monotheism (belief in one God) over polytheism (the belief in many gods). Ancient polytheists typically had few problems with other cultures worshipping other deities. When Cyrus conquered Babylon in the 400s BCE, he had no problem with Babylonians continuing to worship Marduk or Israelites continuing to worship Yahweh. As a good polytheist, Cyrus would likely affirm the existence of these deities and he might as well have his new subjects keeping those deities happy and praying good things about him.

That mindset is altogether foreign to the monotheistic religions of Judaism and Christianity. When a person believes in one—and only one—God, that leaves no room for Zeus, Marduk, Artemis, or anyone else to claim lordship. That would especially go for the popular imperial cult that worshiped the emperor as divine in first century Asia Minor.

The belief in one God who lays claim over all creation—including all nations—had political ramifications when Christians refused to participate in holidays and feasts designed to honor the gods or Caesar. For Christians, such religious observances constituted the essence of idolatry, or split allegiances. Meanwhile those around them viewed Christians as unpatriotic, irreligious (they had no idol to worship), and seditious in their teachings

---

4. DeSilva, *Discovering Revelation*, 41.

about another kingdom that had already been inaugurated in Jesus. When Christians refuse to syncretize their worship with Rome (whether Rome of the first century, or one of the many "Romes" available today), it puts them on a collision course with society at large.

In contemporary North America, this principle is obscured by the assumption that the church and government are separated. Be that as it may, there remains a great pull within Western society to syncretize by combining our worship of Christ with elements of our culture.

An appropriate case and point might be the presence of the American flag in Christian sanctuaries. Many evangelical Christians contemplate leaving their churches when the flag is removed. In almost the same breath as we value the separation of church and state, we are willing to divide when the syncretism of love-for-country and love-for-God is threatened. Very quickly, our politics evoke religious decisions: leaving the church. Revelation might sound the alarm that our allegiance is potentially divided between our nation and Christ. The willingness of some Christians to divide over the issue would tend to confirm that worry.

That is only one example of a dangerous syncretism between the Christian faith and what Michael Gorman calls "civil religion," or religion syncretized with the state.[5] Other examples might include the following:

- Christians's willingness to jettison biblical teachings to secure one's rights.
- Christians who compromise with cultural views on sexuality.
- Christians so certain about their political party's (or candidate's) merit that they speak or portray it as operating under God's sanction (e.g., pictures with Jesus guiding a president's hand while signing an executive order).

Revelation calls the church to "uncivil religion"—not in the sense of "uncivilized," but in the sense of uncontaminated by the worship of anything besides Christ.[6] It is through unswerving loyalty to Jesus alone that the church receives the comforts offered to Smyrna and Philadelphia. This kind of loyalty to Christ may lead to small churches that are very countercultural. This, however, is better than the alternatives that threatened

---

5. Gorman, *Reading Revelation Responsibly*, 40–56.
6. Gorman, *Reading Revelation Responsibly*, 55–56.

the other five churches—when the church compromises and fits in with culture, we receive urgent calls to repentance from Jesus.

10. A Concluding Question

The crucial question that Rev 2–3 leaves for modern readers is "which congregation do we attend?" It is a difficult and convicting question. Everyone wants to attend the "good" churches that receive no condemnation, Smyrna and Philadelphia. The harsh reality, though, is these churches faced the greatest opposition for being countercultural. That being the case, if the church we attend today is at home in its culture, it is far more likely we find ourselves in Sardis or Laodicea. As such, as much as Revelation offers hope, it also calls us to repentance. When we answer that call, we begin to feel external pressures from society and internal pressures from the Jezebels and Baalams who prefer compromise, complacency, and syncretism. Even so, the intent of Revelation is to illustrate that the promises of Jesus to repentant believers far outweigh the trials we shall face.

For Further Study

Discussion Questions

1. Which description of Jesus from the seven letters impacts you the most and why?
2. Which church in Rev 2–3 received the letter you think speaks best to your congregation?
3. The end of the chapter offers examples of syncretism, or "civil religion." Can you think of any other examples?

Table 1
Jesus' Letters to the Seven Churches

	Doing Well	**Doing Wrong**	**Blessing**	**Threat**
Ephesus	Did not tolerate evil people	Forgot their first love	Permission to eat from the tree of life in God's paradise	Removal of their lampstand
	Tested false apostles			
	Endured for Jesus' name			
	Hated the Nicolaitans			
Smyrna	Faithful in tribulation and poverty		Crown of life	
	Truly rich despite appearances		Not harmed by second death	
Pergamum	Held to Jesus' name	Some held to Balaam's teaching (idolatrous meat; immorality)	Given hidden manna	Jesus will make war with the sword of his mouth
	Had not denied Jesus' faith	Held to Nicolaitans' teaching	Given a white stone with a new name	
Thyatira	Their works included faith, love, service, and endurance.	Tolerated Jezebel who does not want to repent from her immorality	Authority to rule nations with a rod of iron.	Those who persist in following Jezebel will receive great tribulation.
	Their recent works were greater than their earlier ones		Given morning star	Jesus will reward everyone for his/her own works
			Jesus will reward everyone for his/her own works	

Encountering Jesus in Revelation

	Doing Well	Doing Wrong	Blessing	Threat
Sardis		They were dead	Given white robes	Jesus will come like a thief
		Their deeds were incomplete	Names written in Book of Life	
Philadelphia	Kept Jesus' word without rejecting his name despite having little power		The synagogue of Satan will pay them homage and know Jesus loves them	
			Kept from a time of testing coming on the whole world	
			Received a crown	
			Received a pillar in the temple	
			Inscribed with God's name, New Jerusalem's name, and Jesus' new name	
Laodicea		Neither hot nor cold; lukewarm	By buying from Jesus they may become rich, clothed, and capable of sight	Jesus will spew them out of his mouth
		Spiritually poor, naked, blind, wretched, and miserable	Jesus will enter and dine with them if they open the door	
			Sit on the throne with Jesus	

5

Heavenly Worship

Preparatory reading:

- Revelation 4–5
- Ezekiel 1
- Listen to these songs on YouTube: "Revelation Song," "Holy, Holy, Holy," and "Agnus Dei"[1]

1. Introduction

The first time I recall sensing God's presence was at a kids' camp while we sang "Lord, I Lift Your Name on High." As I listened to the words of the song—and heard my voice caught up in the chorus of other kids and adults praising God—I sensed that God was real and present.

    Decades later, I had a similar experience. During a worship service at the annual meeting of the Wesleyan Theological Society, I serendipitously sat near several leading theologians within my branch of Christianity. As the obvious misfit among a congregation of people I deeply respected, I tried not to sing off-key in the worship service. Then it happened. I received a taste of heaven as we sang Charles Wesley's words: "Amazing Love! How can it be that Thou, my God, shouldst die for me?"[2] As we sang, the

---

1. Integrity Music, "Revelation Song"; Reawaken Hymns, "Holy Holy Holy"; Smith, "Agnus Dei."
2. Wesley, "And Can It Be?"

voices of men and women much smarter and more reverent than I split into a wondrous four-part harmony. And, for the briefest of moments, I was among the saints worshiping before God. That day, I caught a glimpse of the church doing what it was designed to do: worship.

Experiences like these are a useful frame of reference for reading Rev 4–5, which reports John's vision of a heavenly worship service. It is easy for us to focus on the details: precious stones, symbols, numbers, creatures, sounds, imagery, etc. But as we survey the glorious landscape of heaven, our gaze centers on one place: the throne. Everything else is peripheral, surrounding in worship the one seated on the throne.

2. The Center of Creation (Revelation 4:1–11)

Most of us know the agony of trying to describe something that refused reduction into words. Some experiences cannot be verbalized. I suspect John felt that frustration when penning Rev 4. He witnessed something amazing. He entered God's throne room and watched the cosmos engaged in worship. How does one describe that?

John was in the same boat as Ezekiel, who also attempted to describe an indescribable vision. In exasperation, Ezekiel finally surrendered to the limitations of language saying, "Such was the appearance of the likeness of the glory of the Lord" (Ezek 1:28). John experienced similar difficulty in articulating what he saw. The word "like" appears six times in Rev 4. John couldn't quite describe what he saw, he could only compare it with what readers might know by saying, "It was kind of like. . ."

The first item to capture John's attention was God's throne, the center of gravity for the entire vision. John's gaze fixated on the gemstone-like appearance of the one sitting on the throne surrounded by a shining emerald-like rainbow. Everything else came into view as John's overstimulated eyes adjusted to the brightness and glanced to the sides.

The description of the throne communicates important theological truths. Like any throne, it was the seat of God in his power, from which will issue judgment and salvation (see Rev 7:10; 20:11–12). Encircling this seat of awesome authority, John saw one of the most profound symbols of God's power and faithful love: a rainbow. In Gen 9, the rainbow became the symbol of God's merciful promise never again to flood the earth. Elsewhere in the ancient world, the bow symbolized the power held by divine archers. Even in Genesis, the hanging of the rainbow in the sky implied that God was no longer using it to shoot judgment on earth, like he did in Gen 6–8. Both meanings—God's mercy and power—are appropriate background for the rainbow in Rev 4: God is both almighty and merciful. The rainbow encircles the throne reminding us that God's power and mercy emanate from the throne together.

Conversely, the aura surrounding the throne may not be a rainbow. David deSilva correctly observed that this rainbow has only one color and that the Greek word translated "rainbow"—*iris*—differs from the one used in the Greek translation of Gen 9, which was popular among John's readership.[3] Even so, the range of meanings for the Greek word includes both rainbows, as well as other bright circles such as a halo.[4] If an emerald halo is what John intended to communicate, it would be another means of highlighting the grandeur and majesty of the heavenly throne room.

Moving out from God's throne, John observed twenty-four other thrones that seated twenty-four elders. Whether these elders were humans or God's angelic courtiers does not impact their function within the vision: they represent the twelve tribes of Israel and the twelve apostles. Combined, these groups symbolize the complete people of God. They were clothed in white, which Revelation associates with victory (Rev 7:13–14; 19:11–16) and they wore crowns, perhaps reminiscent of their status as God's kingdom of priests (Rev 1:6; cf. Exod 19:6; 1 Pet 2:5).

In front of the throne, was something described as "a sea of glass like crystal" (Rev 4:6, author's translation), which conjures several intertextual allusions. This sea was the heavenly counterpart to the bronze sea in Solomon's Temple (1 Kgs 7:23–26). In addition to the possible utilitarian purpose of washing, the large basin in Solomon's temple may have symbolized the sea from which creation emerged (Gen 1:2) and the Red Sea through which Israel passed.[5] Of course, to the extent that the temple represents the cosmos correctly oriented around God, it is also appropriate for such a basin to represent the sea as part of God's creation. All of this symbolism underpins the appearance of the sea in Revelation. It is the heavenly counterpart to the physical sea on earth, whose inhabitants worship God (Rev 5:13) even if victimized by spiritual realities (12:12). Likewise, if we read Revelation within the context of the story of God's people, we might remember the Red Sea and conclude that the one seen by John constitutes a

---

3. DeSilva, *Discovering Revelation*, 65.
4. Liddell et al., "Ἶρις," 836.
5. Sweeney, *1 and 2 Kings*, 122.

visual reminder of God's deliverance of his people (this is especially so if it is the same sea readers find in Rev 15:2). Finally, like the basin in Solomon's Temple, the sea in heaven's throne room may also serve as a laver for washing away impurity since sin contaminates even heaven (Rev 12:7; cf. Heb 9:23).

Moving further afield from the throne, John observed four living creatures whose appearance recalled Ezek 1:5–10. There are important differences, however. The four creatures Ezekiel saw were identical: each having four heads resembling a different animal. In Revelation, each living creature was distinct from its counterparts. The meaning of the creatures is variously explained, but one attractive interpretation argues they symbolize God's animate creation: the lion is the mightiest of wild beasts; the ox is the strongest among domesticated livestock; and the eagle soars as king of the birds. Humans also take their place in this order with the third living creature possessing a human face.

These creatures led heaven in unceasing praise and worship of the one sitting on the throne. As they glorified God, the twenty-four elders fell down in worship and threw their golden crowns before him. They cried out, "Worthy are you, our Lord and God, to receive glory and honor and power; for you created all things and through your will they existed and were created" (Rev 4:11, author's translation).

The heavenly court surrounds the creator-God in praise, confessing that he is deserving of worship. Compared to such magnificent glory, the courts of earthly kings become cheap replicas, if not parodies. Caesar too surrounded himself with advisors and enjoyed people singing his praises, but his apparent glory dimmed to invisibility in John's vision of the true King of kings.

Today's Caesars do not fair any better. People aspire to power, attempting to occupy thrones around which others gather in fawning worship of a persona of might, or wealth, or some other characteristic. Successful as our Caesars might appear, Douglas Webster makes an important point about such quests: "Often the height of our aspiration is matched by the depths of our disillusionment."[6] There is only one who wields ultimate authority and who deserves such glory and it is this one that the people of God surround with the anthem, "Worthy are you!"

---

6. Webster, *Follow the Lamb*, 118

3. Who is Worthy? (Revelation 5:1–14)

Inaugurating God's Plan

I type these words on the day of a general election in the United States; a day when the nation will choose its leader for the next four years. Each of the candidates has made grand promises regarding the nation's future prosperity (if they are elected), or doom (if their opponent is elected). As I listen to the rhetoric, I find myself asking the question that echoed down heaven's halls in Rev 5: *who is worthy?*

Who is worthy to receive power? Who can bring peace? Who can legitimately occupy the throne and right everything that is wrong with the world? It is a question that voters will answer today. It was also a question for Christians living under the rhetoric of the *pax romana* (the peace Rome secured by its military might): who is worthy?

As the heavenly worship service of Rev 4 continued, John returned his gaze to the throne and noticed a scroll (many translations say "book") in the hand of the one sitting on the throne. The contents of the scroll are a matter of debate. In other apocalyptic writings, such documents contained God's plan for bringing about his final salvation and judgment (see Dan 12:4; 1 Enoch 81:1–3; 93:1–3). That is the most probable explanation for the scroll of Revelation 5.

God, in his sovereignty, planned how he will accomplish ultimate salvation and do away with evil and injustice once and for all. The plan is so extensive that the scroll had writing on its front and back sides (Rev 5:1), which was unusual in antiquity. What marvelous revelations might the scroll disclose about God and the world?

Almost as quickly as John saw the scroll, he realized it was sealed. Important ancient documents were sealed with wax to guarantee their authenticity. Such was the case here and no one was deemed worthy to remove the seals. John began to weep. He did not simply shed a tear; he was crying uncontrollably—weeping. In my younger days, my reaction to John's response was "what's the big deal?" I have never cried at the inaccessibility of a book. John was distraught because the initial step for enacting God's plan required someone to open the scroll. Alas, no one from the heights of heaven to the depths of the earth and sea approached the throne as worthy to unfurl God's plan. John lamented the suspension of God's saving initiative.

Behold, the Lamb

John rode an emotional roller coaster. Whereas Rev 4 brought the ecstasy of heavenly worship, Rev 5 introduced the depths of despair. As John grieved, one of the twenty-four elders informed him that there *is* one who has claimed victory: the Lion of the tribe of Judah, the root of David; *he* is worthy (Rev 5:5). These titles evoke several Old Testament passages, as well as Jewish literature from the intertestamental period. Isaiah mentioned the root of Jesse (David's father; Isa 11:10), as well as a righteous "Branch" (11:1; cf. Zech 3:8; 6:12). Both titles became symbolic of the Messiah, the king expected to come from David's lineage.

In Jesus, we find God's victorious Messiah. Even better, he is worthy. Amazing as that is, it does not prepare John for what he sees next. Turning around to see this conquering King approach the throne and open the scroll, John witnessed something altogether unexpected. First, he saw no one approaching the throne. John's eyes fixated once again on the throne itself, around which the living creatures symbolizing all creation gathered in praise. In the middle of all that, John saw . . . a lamb. Not a lion; a baby sheep stood at the center of everything. Even more, the lamb had been slaughtered, yet somehow lived.

The slaughtered lamb imagery alludes to the crucifixion of Jesus, the Lamb of God who takes away the sin of the world (John 1:29). As the slaughtered lamb, Jesus still bears the marks of his sacrificial death. He shall ever be the Crucified One. But the Crucified One is also the Living One (Rev 1:18). The resurrection of Jesus vindicated him as God's Messiah. He is the one who—through sacrifice—conquered death and lives forever and ever. This victory for David's descendant marks Jesus not only as the lamb, but also the royal lion of Judah (David's tribe).

The combination of lion and lamb imagery redefines our notions of God's power. Western readers of Revelation typically imagine power in ways reflected in Greek mythology more than the New Testament. For instance, if we translated our conceptions of power into a Greek worldview, we might arrive at a picture of Zeus sitting atop a cloud with a lightning bolt ready to zap our enemies. Of course, parts of Scripture describe Israel's God in similar ways (Ps 59:11–13; Isa 10:12–19; Hab 3:3–15). Nevertheless, the power of the conquering lion in Rev 5:5 is defined by the sacrificial lamb in v. 6.

This raises an important principle for interpreting Revelation: what John sees often interprets what he hears. He has heard of the powerful lion of Judah; what he sees is the sacrificial death and resurrection of Jesus, the Lamb. "Both images point to the same reality."[7] The Messiah came and conquered, but that victory took an unexpected form. The Lamb is not weak; he is victorious and powerful, but victory and weakness are turned upside down by Jesus. The ultimate victory over evil happened on Good Friday, when the wages of sin were paid, and on Easter morning when Jesus rose to make his people righteous (Rom 4:25). That is the paradigm of victory and power for Jesus' followers.

The fact that John saw a lamb on the throne rather than a lion is important. When "the slaughtered lamb is seen 'in the midst of' the divine throne in heaven (5:6; 7:17), the meaning is that Christ's sacrificial death *belongs to the way God rules the* world. The symbol of the lamb is no less a divine symbol than the symbol of 'the One who sits on the throne.'"[8] God won victory through sacrifice. The battle is done, which is why there is no struggle—in any real sense—between God and evil in Revelation. Rather, any battle that involves Jesus is fought by his sovereign word (Rev 2:16; 19:15, 21). The Lion of Judah roars as the God who spoke creation into existence and evil must flee.

The Lamb is also God. His seven horns and eyes symbolize the fullness of God's spirit sent out into the world (Rev 5:6). If we contemplate that point, we see the truth of the symbolism. The church does not witness the power of God in military might. The crusades did not achieve spiritual victory. God's spirit was not at work in murderous campaigns undertaken by European kings and clergy. Where we do see the Holy Spirit at work in our world is in the sacrificial death of countless missionaries and martyrs who brought the gospel to remote parts of the world. We see God's Spirit at work in the Stephens (Acts 6:8—7:60), Pauls, Antipasses (Rev 2:13), Pricillas, Polycarps, and Bonhoeffers. They claimed powerful victories as they followed the Lamb to death and victory.

John watched the Lamb approach and take the scroll from the one on the throne. Most English translations use the simple past tense to report the transfer of the scroll: *he took the scroll*. That is probably the best English translations can do without spending several pages of commentary to speak about the event's significance. What we miss, though, is the nuance of Greek grammar, which places the verb "take" in the perfect tense, "has taken." That tense does much more than communicate what John saw

7. Koester, *Revelation and the End*, 78.
8. Bauckham, *Theology*, 64 (italics in the original).

and when he saw it. Rather, John has used the grammatical equivalent of printing that word in bold and highlighting it. The Lamb *HAS TAKEN* the scroll![9]

Scholars who study Greek grammar have also taught that the perfect tense expresses both (1) that something happened in the past and (2) that the results of that event continue to affect one's present. For example, when one parent says to the other in the wee morning hours, "The baby has wakened," more is being communicated than a past event. The implication is that a new situation has arisen and one must act accordingly. That understanding of the Greek perfect tense has recently been questioned, but contextually Revelation allows us to make the same point about Jesus' receipt of the scroll: he has indeed taken the scroll and inaugurated God's plan of salvation.

Heaven's Response to the Lamb

The comfort Revelation offered early Christians was not that Jesus would someday reign or that he would someday show up in heaven to take control of matters. The Christians of Philadelphia found solace not in Jesus doing something millennia after their bodies disintegrated; their comfort was that Jesus is on the throne now. He reigns as King now. He has taken the scroll and this means his followers must endure faithfully as they follow the lion by walking in the path of the Lamb.

When the Lamb took the scroll, heaven's response was immediate. He was not charged with overweening pride for presuming to approach the throne. Nobody thought this crucified Jesus had stepped out of line. The response from creation (the four living creatures) and from the people of God (the twenty-four elders) was worship (Rev 5:8–10). Once again the central theme of Revelation emerges: worship. The elders fell before the Lamb with incense symbolizing the prayers of the saints. The prayers of the oppressed Christians in Smyrna, and of those who remained faithful in Pergamum even when Antipas died, and of those in Thyatira who resisted Jezebel's teachings, rose in heaven as a sweet aroma when the victorious Christ received what only he can take.

As the incense rose, the elders sang a new song. Revelation 4 painted a picture of unending antiphonal praise. The four living creatures would sing,

---

[9]. See Mathewson, *Revelation: A Handbook*, 75–76.

> Holy, holy, holy is the Lord God Almighty,
> Who was and who is and who is to come.
> (Rev 4:8, author's translation)

And the elders would respond:

> Worthy are you, our Lord and God
> To receive glory and honor and power
> Because you created all things
> And through your will they existed and were created.
> (Rev 4:11, author's translation)

That unending symphony of worship had been interrupted by the angel's question, "Who is worthy to open the scroll?" (5:2, author's translation). Now that Jesus has taken it, a new song echoed through the universe. The elders and living creatures proclaimed:

> Worthy are you to receive the scroll
> And to open its seals
> Because you were slaughtered
> And purchased for God with your blood
> From every tribe and tongue and people and nation . . .
> (Rev 5:9, author's translation)

In response, thousands of angels sang out:

> Worthy is the slaughtered lamb to receive
> Power and riches and wisdom
> And strength and honor and glory and blessing.
> (Rev 5:12, author's translation)

And then all creation in heaven and earth and under the earth and in the sea (everywhere that one worthy to take the scroll had been sought) sang:

> To the one who sits on the throne and to the lamb
> Be blessing and honor and glory and power
> Forever and ever.
> (Rev 5:13, author's translation)

Finally, the four living creatures ended the song: "Amen" (5:14). And the elders continued in worship.

4. Conclusion—Revelation 4–5: The Theological Center of the Book

Revelation 4–5 is crucially important for understanding the entire book. These chapters give the perspective from which readers must watch the coming judgments and the church's struggle with the beast and his minions. The venue in Revelation is not one in which we find ourselves overwhelmed in the chaos and destruction of our world. Rather, our vantage point is heaven and this view anchors the church to hold it firm through the coming storm.

The apocalyptic perspective opened up for the church in Rev 4–5 is one of heavenly worship. We glimpse all creation properly ordered and the people of God—in unity—surrounding the throne in worship. In the midst of that throne we find God seated in power as sovereign over all creation and encircled by the rainbow. We also find that power redefined by the picture of the crucified Jesus who has claimed victory. This Jesus comes and takes the scroll that reveals God's plan for salvation and judgment.

When Jesus does this, all creation glorifies him and proclaims that he is worthy to receive the scroll. That perspective is the centering vision we must retain when reading Revelation.[10] Jesus is at the center of everything and he has claimed victory. He has taken the scroll and is reigning on the throne with the Father.

The only appropriate response to such a vision is worship. The nature of that worship, as well as how we respond to the lion and lamb metaphors in Rev 5, depends on the congregations we attend. What one sees here depends on whether one attends church in Smyrna or Laodicea.

For the suffering Christians of Smyrna to whom Jesus said even more trials were coming, our worshipful response to the glimpse of heaven is colored by the doctrine of Christ (Christology) we find there: he is the conquering lion of the tribe of Judah. Smyrnean Christians are reminded that Jesus is the fulfillment of the people of God's hopes and he is the one who has begun to reign, seated on the throne next to the Father. Our response is to persevere in worshiping him, recognizing that our prayers rise as the incense of God's people before the throne.

For lukewarm Christians at home in the world of Laodicea, our worshipful response to realizing that Jesus has the scroll is a healthy dosage of Lamb-Christology. When we let the Lamb instruct us, we find what

---

10. See Gorman, *Reading Revelation Responsibly*, 102–115.

Dietrich Bonhoeffer explained: "When Christ calls a man, he bids him come and die."[11] Jesus was victorious through sacrifice and he calls us to sacrifice. Thus, our response to Rev 4–5 is to repent because we recognize our comforts have compromised our allegiance to Christ. Our worship is to kick into action and begin living according to the pattern of Jesus.

Wherever we find ourselves, whether it is Smyrna, Laodicea, or elsewhere, Rev 4–5 calls us to proper worship. It reminds us of who truly deserves worship as the gravity of the heavenly throne room draws us away from the idols demanding our allegiance. It is from this place that the judgements to come are issued. Jesus is about to begin to exercise his sovereign lion-like power even as the church is invited to follow the Lamb.

For Further Study

Discussion Questions

1. How does the metaphor of the lamb redefine power and how God's people should understand it?
2. What is your response to the heavenly worship scenes we see in these chapters?
3. If an outside observer were to consider your life, who might that person conclude is the one you believe to be worthy to claim lordship?
4. Watch the video of a rendition of "Is He Worthy" in this link and imagine how John felt as he witnessed these words sung in heaven: https://www.youtube.com/watch?v=aEelKGcPomI

---

11. Bonhoeffer, *Cost of Discipleship*, 89.

6

The Seals

Preparatory reading:

- Revelation 6–7
- Ezekiel 9

1. Introduction

Revelation 4–5 immersed us in the wonder of a heavenly worship service. John saw Jesus, the lion of the tribe of Judah, as the lamb of God slaughtered to purchase his people. Caught up in the unending praise of the four living creatures and the twenty-four elders, John glimpsed creation as it should be: gathered in worship around God's throne.

    After such a sight, we might anticipate that the next scene (Revelation 6) would describe the return of Christ with the scroll and the final glorification of the Lamb. Alas, that is still to come. John's world—our world—is not engaged in worshiping God. Evil persists. Creation is not as it should be; it is in rebellion against the creator and it appears quite content with this situation. Even worse, our world actively works against its creator by afflicting those who follow Jesus (recall the experiences of Christians in Smyrna, Philadelphia, and Pergamum), or by contaminating their worship (Pergamum and Thyatira). Before we can celebrate God's ultimate victory and salvation, a world immersed in sin awaits God's redemptive plan.

That plan, which will bring an end to evil, is written in the scroll of Revelation 5 and it is received and launched by Jesus, the sacrificial lamb victimized by evil. The crucifixion sets the tone for God's redemptive plan by demonstrating that he will not force people out of evil. Jesus does not burglarize the Laodicean church, but stands knocking at the door, waiting to gain entrance. This freedom not to choose God must be remembered when reading the judgments of Revelation, which commence as Jesus breaks the seals on the scroll.

The seal judgments do not force submission to Christ. Instead, they force a choice. When people encounter judgment, their options are (1) to awaken from idolatry and repent, or (2) to entrench themselves in sin. In these judgments, God permits evil to run rampant, showing creation how bad sin is. Perhaps, the bitterness of life without God will leave us thirsting for the living water offered by Jesus.

The following analysis is not a verse-by-verse commentary on God's judgments. Adequate resources have already met that need (see the further reading suggestions at the end of this chapter). Instead, I hope to offer an overarching perspective one might bring to the text, or a lens with which to understand the judgments. Readers must permit each passage to stand on its own, but neither must we lose the forest among the trees. In this chapter, I provide a glimpse of the forest by focusing on the purpose of the judgments and the ensuing worship.

2. Insecurity of a World in Chaos: Seals 1–4 (Revelation 6:1–8)

The purpose of God's judgments in Revelation—most of them, at least—is not *only* to punish sin, but includes a call to repentance. This point is made in Revelation by explicit statements about the failures of judgments to engender repentance and worship through the seals (Rev 6:15–17), the trumpets (9:20–21), and the bowls (16:10–11). Later, we shall see that it is through the faithful witness of God's people that the world begins to glorify God (11:13).

In this chapter, our focus is on the role of the seals, which call creation to repentance as Jesus opens them. The measures taken seem drastic as the four horsemen ride through the world. Indeed, they are drastic measures taken in response to people in places like Thyatira, where the false teacher Jezebel and her followers rebuffed Jesus' warnings. In the seals, those following false teachings (Pergamum and Thyatira) and those who are lethargic in their faithfulness (Ephesus, Sardis, and Laodicea) find opportunities to follow the path charted by the faithful (Smyrna and Philadelphia) by emulating the life of the Lamb. God is seeking to awaken faithfulness within his people.

The first four seals shake people awake by creating insecurity. When the Lamb opened the first seal, John saw a rider on a white horse with a bow. The rider received a crown and went into the world to conquer. Rome's propaganda praised the empire's ability to secure peace through military might. The problem was those on the receiving end of conquest do not experience might as peace. The first rider entered the world reminding people that conquerors always linger and destabilize our security. For Roman readers, the imagery might remind them of their enemies to the east—the dreaded Parthian cavalry with its accomplished archers.

Following conquest comes the second horseman, representing the means by which conquest most often happens: violence and bloodshed. The fiery red horse and its rider rob the world of peace. The peace praised by Rome's propaganda was as an illusion; it was a superficial peace. Perhaps open hostility was occasionally limited to a distant battlefield, but that is not peace. To suggest that it is promulgates the lie that the red horseman shatters his mighty sword.

Whereas conquest and war affect us all, we typically feel them most keenly on the national level. Wars, especially for powerful countries, are something that one's nation can fight "over there." Much closer to home is one's economy. How much do I pay for bread and can I depend on the grocery store having food? This is the third horseman's arena. When this horse rode out, John heard a voice from the midst of the living creatures crying out, "A measure of wheat for a day's wages and three measures of barley for a day's wages, but do not damage the oil or the wine" (Rev 6:6, author's translation). Such prices reflected catastrophic inflation of daily goods even as luxury items like oil and wine remained available.[1] Whether greed or famine created the situation, survival became difficult for ordinary people.

It is difficult to say why the voice in the center of the living creatures called for oil and wine to be preserved. If the phrase points toward early Christian practices of anointing with oil and the sacrament of the Lord's supper, it could indicate the Lamb provides for his people in the midst of famine, but a more simple explanation is that olive trees and vineyards are

---

1. Robert Mounce observed that the prices here are ten to twelve times their ordinary cost (*Revelation*, 144).

not hit as hard by famines as grain crops.[2] Thus, the preservation of these crops indicates a limited scope to the judgment.

Finally, at the end of the lineup, comes the pale horse ridden by Death himself and followed by Hades. In a world where security has evaporated, Death sweeps in to remind us that life itself cannot be taken for granted. The rider received authority to kill a quarter of the earth's inhabitants with hunger, swords, and beasts.

The first four seals are so threatening that many readers of Revelation are content to leave them addressing the first-century church alone. Other readers, perhaps most readers in North America, are at the other end of the spectrum. We allocate these horrifying events to a future date in history and hope we will no longer inhabit the earth when they erupt into history.

Both approaches render Revelation safe for the unfaithful. If I enjoy comfort and complacency while attending Laodicea First Church, understanding the four horsemen as agents of God's judgment in the distant future—or in the days of ancient history—will elicit no change in my life now. Such readers have missed the point. Revelation is not supposed to be safe for the unfaithful. As apocalypse and prophecy, it speaks to the church of now, whenever now might be.

The horsemen of conquest, violence, economics, and death certainly rode through the Roman Empire; they continue to ride in our time as well and will continue to wreak havoc until the Lamb returns. Nations continue to lust for power and conquest. Wars—whether rationalized as just or not—will continue to plague our planet with thousands killed each year by the bloody red sword of the rider on the red horse. Economic downturns continually threaten our security. Stock market crashes and supply chain shortages created by catastrophes (wars, famines, pandemics, etc.) remind us that our resources run thin. And behind it all lurks Death himself who comes for each of us.

In the chaos, it becomes difficult to find meaning. But Revelation supplies meaning to such events by revealing a call return to Christ and the one seated on the throne. Will those who grow weary of chaos turn to the Lamb? Without the perspective of Rev 6, this world becomes a scary place to live. John's vision has placed under the microscope the fearful reality created by our sin. When faith opens our eyes, we find something unexpected: the powers of sin bring chaos, but God—while not ordaining sin—remains faithful to call for our attention through the havoc we endure. The

---

2. Mounce, *Revelation*, 144.

horsemen do not ride with their own authority and their power is limited. Each of them is summoned into the heavenly throne room and none of them has the final word. Their mission is to awaken the world to the effects of sin and its need of our creator and redeemer.

3. Hope and Fear: Seals 5–6 (Revelation 6:9–17)

While the evil results of sin stampede, two more seals portray the possible responses of humanity. On the one hand, we find encouragement and hope; on the other hand is fear and entrenchment in sin.

When the fifth seal opened, John saw the martyrs of the church under heaven's altar. He saw people like Antipas who had died for his testimony about Jesus (Rev 2:13). These victims of sin and injustice pleaded with the God of justice, asking, "How long before you will avenge our blood?" They called for vindication. Like the Lamb, they had been victorious through faithfulness, but their victory—like his—was one of apparent defeat. These martyrs join God's people throughout the ages who await the ultimate righting of what has gone wrong. We hear the cry for justice, the wish for oppressors to receive punishment.

Each of the faithful received a white robe, symbolizing victory. They conquered no less than their evil counterpart on the white horse (Rev 6:2). To the martyrs, however, belongs a true victory. Their victory was no superficial expansion of territory; it was faithfulness to God. They are told to wait until their number is complete. The possibility of victory remains for people who will turn to faithfulness as the horsemen ride. The fifth seal concludes with the grim statement that there are still brothers and sisters in Christ who "are about to be killed" (Rev 6:11, author's translation).

How one responds to that statement depends on the church one attends. For a faithful Christian in Pergamum, the notion that people like Antipas are ultimately vindicated by God offers encouragement and hope. What you hear is that victory for the oppressed remains possible and it is *only a little longer* until God's justice arrives (Rev 6:11). We might suffer in the place where the Nicolaitans lead astray and where Satan occupies his throne, but we find solace in knowing that God's throne is greater and Jesus sustains his people with his manna (Rev 2:12–17).

By contrast, Christians from Sardis could hear something entirely different. When we are comfortable and persecution is altogether foreign to us, Rev 6:11 becomes the height of absurdity. *Christians are about to be killed!* Who in their right mind would accept such a destiny? People in Sardis—with their reputation of being alive and vibrant—will be asking why this is necessary? Why can't we go with the flow of society? These are the middle-class Christians who exclaim, "That's not fair! Why should I suffer? Why should I surrender my rights?" In the security of their comfort, they might even poke fun at those silly Philadelphian Christians who haven't figured out how to profess Christ and live comfortably: "If you enjoy discomfort so much, you suffer on your own. I'm happy where I am, thank you very much." Or, they might commit to prayer for those distant suffering Christians without realizing that they themselves are the ones in need of prayer because Jesus has deemed them to be spiritually dead despite their reputation for life.

In the fifth seal, comfortable Christians learn we have missed an opportunity for union with Christ. The martyrs of the church are victorious in the same way that Jesus is victorious. In this, they enjoy a special union with him. The martyrs have lived out what baptism symbolizes: uniting with Christ in his death and resurrecting to new life. For the Christians of Sardis, the initial five seals are a wake-up call to live what we have confessed in baptism.

Whereas the fifth seal portrayed the church's response to evil in our world, the sixth seal reveals what everyone else sees. When the Lamb broke the sixth seal, changes occurred in the sun and moon, stars fell from the sky, and a massive earthquake rumbled. It is important to remember the symbolic nature of what John describes (both here and in the rest of the seals). A literal reading of Rev 6:12-14 will not suffice. Stars cannot fall to earth; even small stars would entirely envelop and incinerate our small planet.

Instead, John describes the cosmic significance of God entering creation. The Old Testament employed similar language to speak of God coming in judgment. Joel mentioned the sun turning dark and the moon becoming blood (Joel 2:31). Amos said the day of the Lord (judgment day) would be a day of darkness, not light (Amos 5:18). Likewise, in the Old Testament earthquakes commonly accompanied God's arrival in judgment (see Isa 13:13; Jer 4:24-26; Nah 1:5; Hag 2:6-7). Because of the metaphorical language in the Old Testament, some suggest that Rev 6 is likewise metaphorical. Perhaps the chaos created by sin is part of how God judges sin. In other words, while massive earthquakes and "stars" falling to earth may or may not happen, we can expect God's judgment will bring the sort of chaos indicative of the four horsemen.

Whether the imagery of Rev 6 is literal (earthquakes and astronomical signs) or metaphorical (a time of great social and political upheaval), or both, the takeaway remains the same: God's action is far-reaching and devastating when he comes to undo evil. The benefit of the metaphorical reading is that we can see God's judgment at work today in times of upheaval. The wrath of the Lamb has come and calls people to repentance.

But even if Rev 6 is read in a more literal manner, the turmoil of earth-shattering events like the Holocaust; Nagasaki and Hiroshima; September 11, 2001; genocidal conquests; wars; and the global pandemic of 2020 along with the economic and supply chain issues that followed should certainly remind us that God calls people to repentance. The day of the Lord is coming and the Minor Prophets were quite clear that this day is one of darkness and judgment. Evil must be rectified. The challenge of Rev 6 is to avoid the response of the earth's inhabitants (Rev 6:15–16). Instead of repentance those in power hid and called for the mountains to fall on them because that appeared a better alternative than enduring the sight of the one seated on the throne and the anger of the Lamb. With Malachi 3:2 they ask, "Who can stand?"

4. Who Can Stand? (Revelation 7)

John's hasty narration of the first six seals prepares us to expect the seventh to follow quickly. Finally—we sense—we will be through the seals and can read the scroll. Alas, John holds us in suspense a bit longer.

In Rev 7, the action pauses. The story is interrupted as John witnessed four angels poised to release destroying winds on the earth and sea. Before that happened, however, another angel announced God's servants must receive a seal on their foreheads. John heard that the ones sealed numbered 144,000 from the tribes of Israel and he turned and beheld a great and innumerable multitude from every nation clothed in white and worshiping God.

The identification of the two groups—the 144,000 and the innumerable multitude—is a flash point among interpreters of Revelation. Commentators who adhere to a dispensational framework (popularized in such books as *Left Behind*) insist these are two distinct groups: the 144,000 being a remnant of faithful Jews whereas the second group consists of Christians of one brand or another. This is certainly an intelligent, simple, and literal reading of Rev 7.

A difficulty, however, is the larger context and theology of Revelation. As we saw in the letters to Smyrna and Philadelphia, Revelation does not drive a wedge between the church and Israel. In its doctrine of the people of God, there is only one people that is composed of Jews and gentiles. For John, and the New Testament, Israel is the Israel that worships the Messiah, and gentiles have been grafted into this people by the grace of God (Rom 11:17–24).

This is why many recent commentators believe the two groups in Rev 7 are one and the same, portrayed from two different angles. This view has much to commend it, but either way we must contemplate how John describes the two groups.

The Metaphors of Revelation 7

The Sealed 144,000 and Its Old Testament Background

Our inquiry into the identity of the two groups can begin with their descriptions. In Rev 7:4, John mentioned the 144,000 were sealed from the twelve tribes of Israel. Interestingly, the list of the twelve tribes omits Dan and Ephraim. Jewish tradition contemporaneous with John suggested the anti-Messiah (Greek: antichrist) would rise from the tribe of Dan. Dan was also the tribe that failed to occupy its territory in Judg 1 and consequently migrated north and squeezed itself in at the very northern point of Israel (Judg 1:34–36; 18:1–31). That move positioned the tribe as among the first to fall when nations like Assyria and Babylon attacked from the north.

Ephraim also had its share of problems. It became the backbone of the Northern Kingdom of Israel and as such was used by the prophets as an alternate name for that kingdom, which had rebelled from the rule of David's heirs. Israel was apostate in its worship; none of its kings were positively evaluated in 1–2 Kings and the remnants of that kingdom (the Samaritans) had intermarried with foreign peoples during the exile. As such, they were regarded as impure by Jews and their worship was suspect as well (they had their own temple and never reintegrated with Judaism). The background of apostasy and prophetic critique likely plays into the omission of both tribes in Rev 7:5–8.

The twelve tribes that do appear receive a mark on their foreheads (Rev 7:3). In light of how much attention and fear the mark of the beast generates among readers of Revelation (see Rev 13:16–18), it is fascinating that the mark of God receives minimal consideration. The act of sealing serves two functions. First, it identifies the one bearing the seal as belonging to God (just as the one bearing the beast's mark identifies an individual who worships him). Secondly, and more importantly for the purposes of Revelation 7, the seal is a mark of protection.

Ezekiel 9:1–11 provides an example of seals functioning in this way. In that passage, God's angelic executioners had to wait until an angel had marked the forehead of those who lamented over the sin that was prevalent among God's people (Ezek 9:4). By the same token, those sealed in Rev 7:4–8 are the faithful whom God protects from the angels ready to release the four winds (Rev 7:1). Whether they are exclusively Jews or whether they symbolize the entire people of God is a matter of debate; their faithfulness, though, is not in question.

Interpreting the 144,000

Interpreting the 144,000 is a highly contested enterprise in the study of Revelation. Regardless of what kind of significance one assigns to this group, taking a position is one way to ensure someone will disagree with you.

Perhaps the simplest route of interpretation is to read the text on a so-called "literal" level and to conclude that the 144,000 arise from ethnic Israel. As noted above, this theory is commended by its simplicity and coherence. Nevertheless, it has some deficiencies. Literal interpretations must allow consideration of an author's intent. If a writer intends something to be read as symbol or metaphor, a literal interpretation must follow that intent. Consequently, if it could be demonstrated that the 144,000 are symbolic in some fashion, it would follow that a literal interpretation must also account for that symbolism. Failure to do so is "overly literal."

An overly literal approach to the 144,000 creates several difficulties. First, equating these with "ethnic Israel" will not do because the census in Rev 7 has made clear that certain parts of Israel are omitted (Dan and Ephraim). Secondly, as already mentioned, the larger context of Revelation's doctrine of God's people points away from dividing Jewish believers and non-Jewish believers. It may be that Rev 7 is an aberration that is theologically inconsistent with Rev 1–6 and 8–22, but this begins to sound like special pleading. It is more probable that the reason for an apparent inconsistency is a misinterpretation of the 144,000.

The Old Testament background of Ezek 9 also pushes against an overly literal reading of the 144,000. Understanding the Old Testament is perhaps the most important interpretive key for reading Revelation. In Ezek 9, God sealed his people who lamented over the prevalence of sin. The point of the sealing was not to identify a special elect group within Israel, but to identify the faithful. Rather than ethnicity, the primary lens through which Ezekiel and Revelation evaluate people is faithfulness: are people faithful, or are they not? Neither book places much emphasis on subdividing God's people.

Be that as it may, Revelation is also unlike Ezek 9 when it lists twelve tribes and rather repetitively states that 12,000 are sealed from each tribe. That sort of repetitiveness echoes the censuses of the Old Testament in Num 1:20–46 and 26:1–51. These censuses were not conducted to assign congressional seats or even to determine tax levels; their purpose was to assess how many men were old enough for combat, which is why they disregard anyone younger than twenty (Num 1:18; 26:4; cf. the military-focused results for David's census in 2 Sam 24:1–9).

That military function of the census may also appear in Revelation. Significantly, Rev 7 is not the only place where the 144,000 appear. We also find them in Rev 14:1–4, where they stand alongside Jesus as an army that John says was "purchased from amongst the earth" (14:4). That language parallels Rev 5:9, which also describes an ethnically diverse group in terms akin to the multitude in Rev 7:9. Each text speaks more broadly about God's people than Jewish believers alone. Consequently, if the 144,000 in Rev 14 represent all believers in the Messiah, it is very possible that the 144,000 in 7:4–8 function similarly. Gregory Beale follows this reasoning when he concludes that the great multitude in 7:9 "is a picture interpreting the number which has been heard in 7:4–8."[3]

A final piece of information worth considering is the number, 144,000. Numbers are often symbolic in Revelation, especially large and round ones. No ordinary census would find exactly 12,000 in each of the tribes of Israel. This on its own can commend a symbolic reading. John's readers could easily have taken the multiplication of twelve by twelve as symbolic for the entirety of God's people. We have has already seen something similar with the twenty-four elders. In Rev 7:4–8, rather than adding the twelve apostles and twelve tribes, John multiplied them and produced the number 144. To

---

3. Beale and Campbell, *Revelation: A Shorter Commentary*, 149.

further emphasize the notion of completion, he multiplied that figure by one thousand.

Given the above lines of evidence, it remains difficult to nail down a firm conclusion about the identity of the 144,000. This is a place to value humility on our part as readers of Scripture. Even well-supported and viable interpretations can be wrong. All of that being said, I see the balance of the evidence pointing toward the 144,000 as a symbolic representation of God's people (including both Jewish and non-Jewish believers). John sees God's people through the lens of the Old Testament and consequently they are symbolized by the twelve tribes squared and multiplied by one thousand. They are the great army that follows the Lamb that we encounter in Rev 14.

A permutation of this position concludes that the 144,000 represent the martyrs. If so, there would be a nice connecting point with the fifth seal, where the martyrs of the past were told to expect more to complete their number. Understanding the 144,000 as martyrs is especially prominent among those who believe Rev 7:1–14 envisions one people of God. This would mean, then, that within the one people of God is a subset of 144,000 who receive special status as the persecuted martyrs. This may be, but the present writer nevertheless believes the 144,000 and the great multitude (see below) are one and the same without further subdivision within God's people.

The Function of the Seal

Regardless of how one answers the "who" of the 144,000, a question about the "what" of the seal remains. The seal provides protection, but is that protection physical or spiritual? Some, citing apocalyptic works roughly contemporaneous with Revelation, believe a physical protection is extended by God before his final judgment.[4]

Others look to the larger context of Revelation to understand the nature of God's protection. When doing this, it becomes difficult to maintain an escapist theology that protects God's people physically. Outside Rev 7:1–4, the best place to look for such a belief is the letter to the Philadelphian church in which Jesus promised to keep the faithful from an hour of testing (2:10). Be that as it may, if Jesus' promise meant removal from the trying situation, it remains difficult to understand why his following exhortation

---

4. Aune, *Revelation 6–16*, 443–44.

presupposed persecution: "Hold firmly to what you have so that no one will take your crown" (2:11).

For the Philadelphian church, the preservation Jesus extended in the time of trial was not removal from persecution but his act of keeping them faithful in the midst of it. The same may be said of the sealing in Revelation 7:4. This is not a promise that God's faithful people (or some subset thereof) will find themselves exempt from trials, temptations, and suffering. Rather, it is a promise of spiritual protection for those who persevere in following the Lamb. Eugene Boring said it well: "Faithful Christians are preserved through (not from!) the great persecution."[5]

The Innumerable Multitude

After hearing the number of those sealed, John saw a great crowd that no one could count that consisted of people from every nation, tribe, people, and language (Rev 7:9). These stood before the Lamb clothed in white and waved palm branches. They joined the heavenly worship service of chapter 4 and praised God and the Lamb for salvation. In response to the praise, the four living creatures, the twenty-four elders, and the angels of heaven fell before God in worship.

One of the twenty-four elders explained that the members of the great multitude were those who came from the tribulation who washed their garments and made them white in the Lamb's blood (Rev 7:14). As such they live in God's presence and worship him. God dwells in their midst and cares for them and the Lamb is their shepherd.

Just as the 144,000 connected to the people of God's history in the Old Testament, the innumerable multitude likewise recalls God's promise to Abraham that all the families of the earth would be blessed through him (Gen 12:3). The children of Abraham would outnumber the sand on the seashore and the stars in the sky. In the New Testament, God's promise to Abraham is applied to all who are in Christ (Rom 9:7–8; Gal 3:6–9, 29).

As the faithful who are in Christ, the members of this multitude wear white robes (Rev 7:9). A few verses later, one of the elders clarifies that the whiteness of the robe is metaphorical: it comes from the blood of the Lamb (Rev 7:14). Anyone who contemplates the text immediately recognizes that blood does not bleach anything white. This is a reference to the purifying

---

5. Boring, *Revelation*, 128.

effect of the blood of Jesus. It is the truth we proclaim in Robert Robinson's hymn, "Come, Thou Fount of Every Blessing":

> Jesus sought me when a stranger,
> Wandering from the fold of God.
> He, to rescue me from danger,
> Interposed his precious blood.[6]

The blood of the Lamb imparts the righteousness of Christ to his followers. It washes them clean and so they are clothed in the white robes of victory as they worship God in spiritual purity. These people are also the beneficiaries of God's provision. They neither hunger nor thirst and the sun does not scorch them. They follow the Lamb as their shepherd and he lovingly wipes the tears from their eyes.

Because of John's explicit claim that this crowd stems from many different ethnicities (7:9), most interpreters agree that this refers to the church in some sense. The question is whether Revelation construes the church as distinct from Israel at this point. If this crowd does in fact consist of people from every people-group, surely Israel should be included. With that observation, it is now appropriate to consider how the great crowd and the 144,000 might be one and the same people.

Two Groups, or One?

As suggested above, there are reasons to conclude the two groups in Rev 7 each symbolize the one people of God. Even so, modern readers can struggle to grasp why Revelation would symbolize one people in two different ways. Readers today often desire one symbol to correspond to one reality, ancient readers and writers did not hold that expectation. In chapter 2, we found that symbols are fluid in apocalyptic literature and often refuse a sort of one-to-one reduction to reality. For instance, in the Shepherd of Hermas one reality—the church—simultaneously appeared as both a tower and a woman with no apparent contradiction perceived by the writer (see discussion in chapter 2).

Similarly, John experienced no difficulty employing multiple symbols for one person or people. In fact, he has already done so. Revelation 5 announced Jesus as the Lion of the tribe of Judah (5:5), but when John turned around, what he saw did not correspond to what he had heard. The same

---

6. Robinson, "Come, Though Fount."

reality (Jesus) was simultaneously symbolized as a lion (5:5) and a lamb (5:6). Neither symbol should be isolated from its counterpart, both are true. In Rev 5, what John saw interpreted what he heard. The imagery of the lamb qualified and defined the way in which the Messiah became the victorious Lion of Judah.

Revelation 7 uses its symbols in exactly the same manner to depict God's people. What John heard interprets what he saw. In v. 4, John *heard* the number 144,000. That auditory experience is interpreted by the visual one: the innumerable multitude. Both pictures correspond to one reality: God's people

In Rev 7:1–17, that people appears in two separate locations. The sealed 144,000 appear on earth and this is the reason for their sealing. On earth, God's people need protection from the menacing winds of vv. 1–3. This reflects the experience of Christians in places like Thyatira and Smyrna. The faithful followers of the Lamb constitute a small remnant facing the onslaught of imperial persecution and the woes accompanying God's judgment on the earth. These are sealed with spiritual protection. We remember the memorable words of Jesus: "In this world, you will have trouble. But take heart! I have overcome the world" (John 16:33 NIV).

By contrast the great crowd of Rev 7:9–17 is not located on earth. They stand before the throne (Rev 7:9). As such, they answer the question posed by the world's powerful people in Rev 6:15–17. Who can stand before the Lamb? The innumerable crowd that recognizes Jesus as their shepherd (7:9, 17).

The crowd appeared in heaven worshiping the one seated on the throne and praising his salvation. These need no seal since they stand in the presence of God. This is an alternative apocalyptic perspective offered by Revelation to struggling faithful Christians. Whereas the situation of the Philadelphian or Pergamene Christians could appear very bleak, the reality they must call to mind is the truth that they worship before the throne.

Furthermore, this worship is included within the ongoing praise of Rev 4. The entities engaged in worship in chapter four now reemerge. When God's people in the crowd cry out, "Salvation to our God who sits on the throne and to the Lamb," we find the twenty-four elders, the angels, and the four living creatures responding: they all fall down and worship God around the throne proclaiming, "Amen! Blessing, and glory, and wisdom, and thanksgiving, and honor, and power, and strength be to our God forever and ever. Amen" (Rev 7:12, author's translation).

5. Conclusion

Revelation 6–7 has taken us on quite a roller coaster. The first four seals unleashed chaos and destruction. We heard the martyrs calling out for justice as plagues and wars struck the earth. Then, in Rev 7, we caught glimpses of God's people, who experience trials and struggles on earth, but also join in the heavenly worship around the throne.

Regardless of the precise meaning one ascribes to the initial six seals, their purpose was to afflict comfortable Christians and to comfort afflicted Christians. As the horsemen ride, the faithful church encounters trials and struggles in a world that is not its home. Even so, Revelation reminds readers that the Lamb is on the throne and is opening God's plan of salvation. Conversely, when the church gets too comfortable in a world that should not be its home, those same horsemen remove security, awaken us from idolatry, and call us back to the Lamb.

For Further Study

Discussion Questions

1. In what ways do you see the horsemen—or maybe echoes of them—riding in our world today?
2. Do you find your response to societal upheaval to be more akin to the response of the martyrs in the fifth seal, or the response of world leaders in the sixth seal? Why do you think that is?
3. Which picture of the church from Rev 7 resonates most with you at this stage of your life?
4. If the 144,000 represent the church, that means faithful Christians are sealed by God. What does this communicate to you about his love and protection?

For Further Reading

- Aune, David. *Revelation 6–16*. Word Biblical Commentary. Vol. 52B. Dallas: Word, 1998.
- Reddish, Mitchell. *Revelation*. Smyth & Helwys Bible Commentary. Macon, GA: Smyth & Helwys, 2001.

7

The Trumpets

Preparatory reading:

- Revelation 8–9
- Exodus 7:1–12:36
- Joel 1:1–7, 13–20; 2:1–17

1. Introduction

In community college, I took Introduction to Psychology and found the subject matter extremely fascinating. I especially enjoyed learning the early history of the discipline when psychologists began to discover the complexities of the human brain by developing creative experiments. In one such experiment, a psychologist studied the results of severing the nerves that connect the left and right hemispheres of the brain. Through the experiment he learned that people were unable to describe or draw what they saw with their left eye when the two hemispheres of the brain became unable to communicate.

Revelation can create that sensation of disconnection as it portrays of two very different worlds. Of course, there is contact between the two pictures, but the differences so far outweigh the similarities that it is almost as though something has severed the connection. Earth operates according to its own paradigm and heaven does likewise. Revelation 8–9 begins where chapter 7 left off: a glimpse of heaven. But it quickly shifts its focus to a very different situation on earth when another series of judgments erupts.

2. The Seventh Seal (Revelation 8:1–5)

As John witnessed the opening of the seals on the scroll, each seal occasioned an awesome event. John watched as horrific horsemen rampaged through the world bringing death and destruction (seals 1–4). He saw God's saints crying for justice and a cataclysmic earthquake that shook people to the point of pleading for mountains to fall on them (seals 5–6). Then, John watched God seal a people for salvation and saw the response of worship when an innumerable multitude gathered around the throne.

In Rev 8:1, Jesus opened the final seal so that the scroll containing God's plan might finally unroll. Everything has built up to this point. As the seal broke, a tangible hush fell over heaven. It was not the kind of silence you hear when nothing is going on; it was the pregnant silence experienced during those monumental points in life when you watch the world change before your eyes. It was the silence that accompanies the gravity of an epoch-changing event when words do no justice to the situation.

The Lamb opened the final seal and nobody dared say a word or do anything for half an hour. Then, John noticed seven angels standing before God's throne who received seven trumpets that would announce a new series of judgments. God's plan of salvation and judgment would continue to unfold.

Before the story continued, though, John spied another angel with a golden censer beside the altar. There, in God's presence, the angel burned incense that consisted of the prayers of the saints (Rev 8:3; cf. 5:8). Prior to the arrival of God's justice, the continuous praise of heaven now paused, creating space for the prayers of God's people to come before him. Included here are the prayers of the martyrs from Rev 6:10 who called out for justice. The world is not as it should be and God's people cry out with the words of lament: "How long, O Lord!"

This is the cry of people whose faith looks to heaven even as they inhabit a horrific dystopia. The seventh seal connects both realities. The setting of John's vision remains in heaven, where the Lamb shepherds his people and wipes the tears form their eyes—this is creation properly ordered. But the prayers of the saints do not arise out of a properly ordered creation; it is a dysfunctional one. The world in which the church finds itself is idolatrous and refuses to recognize its creator. This deep dysfunction must be remedied for God's salvation and justice to prevail.

The problem with dysfunctionality, though, is that it becomes normal to those living with it. That is the struggle of many counselors, pastors, and social workers as they endeavor to help families. Sometimes, dysfunction is all people know and the prospect of leaving that for what is truly healthy becomes excruciating. Correcting dysfunction is painful and that is the project continued by the trumpets in response to the prayers of the church for justice and salvation. God's judgment of evil is painful, but evil must be rooted out and idols must be identified if wholeness is to replace dysfunctionality.

3. Cycles of Sevens (Revelation 8:6)

Before hearing the trumpets, we must consider their relation to the seals. This requires serious thought and reflection for which a metaphor might assist us. When I was in grade school, our family had a microscope that my mother used to teach me and my sisters science lessons. Each lens on the microscope had a different magnification that offered increasingly deeper pictures of whatever we chose to study.

Those different microscope lenses might aid us in understanding the sequences of sevens in Revelation. People often read the narrative of Revelation in a linear fashion: the seals transpire, the trumpets follow, and then the bowls occur before God's final salvation. While straightforward, this method of reading Revelation flounders with the overlap between each sequence. For example, the sixth seal blackened the sun and caused the stars to fall to earth, which sounds like the end of these luminaries (Rev 6:12–13). Nevertheless, they make encore appearances in the fourth trumpet (8:12). Similarly, God's kingdom seemingly arrives with the seventh trumpet (Rev 11:15–19), but then we have more judgments in chapter 16. What's going on here?

The difficulty is on our side of the equation as readers. Western Christians sometimes assume Revelation offers a step-by-step outline of the end times. That's what we expect, so that's what we see when we read. Revelation, however, is more concerned with giving different pictures of a complex reality: sin and our need for salvation. Because each picture portrays the same reality in a different manner, it might be helpful to heed N. T. Wright's words and consider the differences between "writing something with words and writing it with music. In music, you can have several lines which all happen at the same time."[1] With that in mind, think of the different sequences of judgments in Revelation as reporting of the same

---

1. Wright, *Revelation for Everyone*, 63.

events in different ways. In other words, the cycles of Revelation are more like a musician hitting different notes on a piano simultaneously—playing chords—than a sequential narration of what happened when.

Or, to use the microscope analogy, the cycles of judgments are akin to the different lenses. We began with the seals and the removal of security even as God sealed a people for salvation. With the trumpets, the microscope power has increased with a new lens. We behold the same sinful world at a deeper level. Thus, whereas the fourth horseman received power to kill one fourth of the world (Rev 6:8), the new magnification level of the trumpets reveals plagues that torment a third of creation (Rev 8:1–12). Later, the bowls will provide a still deeper look at sin when God's judgment touches all of creation (see Rev 16).

4. Trumpets 1–4 (Revelation 8:7–12)

The image of the trumpet is significant. Trumpets can feature in worship and praise, but in Revelation they often symbolize a warning call. What we should imagine, then, are not the cheerful tones of trumpeters playing Bach's Brandenburg Concertos, but the shrill alarm Israel's prophets associated with the sounding of the ram's horn (cf. Jer 4:19, 21; Hos 5:8–9; Joel 2:1). The trumpets of Revelation herald the day of the Lord that, from the perspective of this world's dysfunction, becomes a day of darkness and judgment, not light and salvation (see Amos 5:18–20).

All of that being said, Rev 8–9 never equates the trumpets with judgment or punishment. To be certain, they fill that role and are perceived as such by the vast majority of people. Nevertheless, the trumpets are more than judgment of sin. Like a microscope, they assist the theological pathologist in identifying sin for what it is, which reveals our need for healing.

Once the trumpets place sin under the microscope, judgment proceeds rapidly. God's people had called out for his justice and salvation and God now grants that request as his power comes crashing into the broken creation. Throughout this sequence, we will find many parallels to the plagues of Exodus. This is because the two sets of judgments share a common purpose: in both Exodus and Revelation God addressed sin while also offering opportunities to repent.

The initial four trumpets proceed quickly. With the first trumpet, John saw hail mixed with blood pummeling the earth. It resembled the hail and thunder of Exod 9:13–35. Unlike in Exodus, however, this plague was not limited to one country. Rather, it destroyed a third of the vegetation throughout the earth (Rev 8:7).

The second trumpet echoed the plague that bloodied the Nile. In Revelation, though, it is a third of the ocean that becomes bloody and kills a third of the things living in the sea. The destruction of the boats worldwide (Rev 8:9) reminds us that there is more going on in Revelation than a literal reading would suggest. Bloodied water does not sink ships. Rather, the blood and fire point to God's judgment on a sinful creation. That judgment now sounds against anything associated with the ocean and one-third of the sea creatures and boats reap the wages of sin.

Some suggest the burning mountain hurled into the sea draws on Jer 51, which depicts judgment with similar imagery (Jer 51:25, 63–64; cf. Rev 8:8). Perhaps that passage provided some imagery, but there are too many differences between the passages to make much of the comparison. In Jeremiah 51, Babylon is the object of God's judgment, not the sea. Another possibility for understanding the mountain in Rev 8 draws on world history from John's time. Around twenty years prior to the writing of Revelation, the eruption of Mt. Vesuvius buried Pompeii and Herculaneum, killing thousands. John may have refashioned this burning mountain as an instrument of God's judgment.

With the third trumpet, a great flaming star named Wormwood fell on a third of the fresh water sources. As with other stars in Revelation, it is probably best to understand the imagery as symbolic of an angel (cf. Rev 1:20; 2:1; 9:1). After all, a literal star would not fall upon the earth; it would envelop it. Again, Jeremiah is a helpful place to look for interpreting Revelation. In Jer 23:13–15, God punished Israel's sin by feeding them wormwood as punishment for Israel's spiritual adultery instigated by false prophets. In Revelation, God accomplishes the same task. Sin had polluted the world and Wormwood arrived to expand on the second trumpet: not only were the oceans polluted, but also the fresh water systems of the world. In both trumpets, we taste the bitterness of sin when it comes under God's judgment.

The sun already went black with the sixth seal (Rev 6:12). Now, with the fourth trumpet, its light is diminished by one-third, along with the moon and stars. This progression indicates that a linear reading of Revelation is not necessarily the best option. Rather, the trumpets apparently sound simultaneously with the seals. This is the same event, but the microscope lens has changed and we now investigate just how deeply sin and idolatry have infected God's creation. The partial darkening of the sun indicates that we are not yet at the final judgment. Time remains for the church and world to turn toward the Lamb. However, like Pharaoh with the plague of darkness (Exod 10:27–28), the world does not express interest in repentance that turns one from darkness to light.

The concept of darkness in the fourth trumpet forms a natural transition to the following judgments in chapter nine. Whereas the natural world is the primary focus point in the first four trumpets, the fifth and sixth trumpets take a turn toward the demonic: locusts will arise out of the black smoke of the abyss and armies of the horsemen will bring death. Spiritual darkness is coming.

As with the Egyptian plagues, the initial trumpet blasts challenge our world's allusions of control. Pharaoh believed he and his gods held sovereignty over Egypt; Rome and its gods believed likewise. Modern Westerners are more atheistic in our worldview, but this only means we look to ourselves—or perhaps nature—as sovereign. Or, if not these, we might propose a principle of randomness governs history—a principle that looks oddly similar to what ancient writers personified as the pseudo-god, "Fortune" or "Chance."

Whatever the case, the first trumpets challenge these illusions of sovereignty as God demonstrates his power and judgment of sin. The natural world, immersed in rebellion against the creator, finds itself under Revelation's microscope and readers can detect a spiritual problem. That problem will become even more visible in the next two trumpets.

5. Trumpets 5-6 (Revelation 8:13—9:19)

Four trumpets have heralded judgment of the natural world. Oceans, rivers, and heavenly bodies suffered as the shrill of the trumpets called the church to faithfulness and the world to repentance. Before proceeding to the fifth trumpet, we find an interruption in the storyline. For a moment, readers breathe between judgments, but that pause is not necessarily comforting.

John heard an angelic eagle call out, "Woe! Woe! Woe!" The call was a warning of the ruin that would accompany the remaining trumpets. Things would only worsen for those on the earth. To use the language of Job: it is "gird-your-loins" time because things are about to get really, really bad.

The Fifth Trumpet

When the fifth trumpet sounded, readers learned why the angel cried out "woe!" John's vivid depiction of the demon-locusts has captivated the imaginations of readers for generations. The locusts strike terror into anyone at the mercy of these merciless tormentors.

It began with an unnamed angel whose origin remains unclear. The description of the angel as a star fallen from heaven could suggest a demonic identity, perhaps even the king of the locusts (see Rev 9:11). When the angel opened the shaft of the abyss, an ominous sign appeared: smoke—black smoke that darkened the sun and sky. It is the kind of smoke one sees from a distance and knows that something has gone horribly wrong (see Rev 18:9–10, 15–19).

Legitimizing the smoke-induced fear are the locusts that emanate from it. These have been variously explained over the years. One writer in the early 1970s associated them with helicopters flying into Vietnam. Such misreadings should caution us against too quickly associating John's visions with current events.

Method is important to our interpretation of Scripture. Sensationalist readings of Revelation typically adopt a method of interpreting John's imagery that moves forward from John's time to our own (or even our future), thereby creating readings of the Scripture that would have been unintelligible to John and meaningless to anyone reading Revelation in the first two millennia of its existence. Remembering that the purpose of apocalyptic literature is to speak to the church of "now"—whenever "now" might be—a better method for understanding Revelation is to move backward from John's time into the Old Testament, which served as the source for the book's imagery. Whereas helicopters and nuclear warheads were unfathomable to John and the Old Testament writers, locusts were a very real terror. As such, two noteworthy Scriptures for our purposes are Exod 10:12–20 and Joel 1–2.

In Joel 2, a locust swarm provided an opportunity to call people to repentance and fasting. It became a chance to recognize the need for God. The response of the people in Rev 9, however, resembled the events of Exod 10, where God's judgment resulted in recalcitrance instead of repentance. As Pharaoh's heart hardened, people today likewise resist repentance. Likewise, the locusts of Revelation torment people and ultimately lead them away from God; they prefer death.

Such is the work of Apollyon (Rev 9:11). This word—and its Hebrew equivalent—means "Destruction" or "Destroyer." By naming the king of the locusts "Destruction," John may be identifying Satan or some other high ranking demon as the culprit. A double, or perhaps alternate, meaning recognizes the similarity between the names Apollyon and Apollo (the Greek war deity). The cult of Apollo was prominent in the Roman world and one of the symbols of Apollo was the locust.[2] Even more interesting is the Emperor Domitian's identification of himself as the human manifestation of Apollo. This being the case, the appearance of Apollyon in Rev 9 might very well constitute a subtle indictment of Apollo's religious establishment, the imperial cult, or even the emperor himself.

All of this points to a clash of sovereignties. The Lamb is on the throne and is the one worthy of glory and praise and honor, but those who are not sealed for salvation have refused to worship him. They believe they themselves, or their idols (government, desires, drugs, money, sex, etc.), possess authority. The locusts expose the false claims of those who would try to rule in place of the Lamb. Idols offer no protection from God and those following idols are subjected to torment while also receiving the opportunity to recognize the Lamb's authority and repent (as some people in Egypt did when they joined Israel in the exodus, see Exod 12:38).

The locusts seem to create an opportunity for repentance, but what do they represent? What is the torment they inflict? Is it spiritual, emotional, physical, or a combination of each? How these creatures might manifest themselves is exceedingly difficult to determine, but a good starting place is to recognize their unique status within Scripture. Unlike locusts in the Old Testament, the ones in Rev 9 attacked people instead of vegetation.

The locusts receive that ability from the same individual who gave the angel the key to the abyss—God (see Rev 9:1). The one who sits on the throne and the Lamb possess ultimate authority. Jesus holds the keys to death and Hades (Rev 1:18). In the fifth trumpet, we find that God's sovereignty extends not only to the earth and natural world, but also to the underworld from which these locusts originate. In John's understanding of the cosmos, the realm of the dead lied beneath the earth. The Old Testament labeled that domain *Sheol*; in Greek culture, it was Hades. It was a place of nonexistence, or at least no meaningful existence. In Revelation, this was also the realm from which demons come and torment those who do not have God's seal (see Rev 11:7; cf. Rev 7:3–4; 20:1–3, 7).

2. Reddish, *Revelation*, 179.

All of this being said, the question remains: *what are the locusts?* This is a place where readers of Revelation must exercise humility and recognize we do not possess all knowledge. Knowing our limitations, we should resist too quickly identifying one event or another with God's judgment or the arrival of the infamous locusts. Even so, the biblical writers encourage us to hear God's call to follow him at the turn of every page of history. This is why Wright also cautions against too quickly dismissing catastrophes as a way God deals with iniquity. He says,

> We, too, have seen terrible things in our day: monsters, whether helicopters or other military equipment, designed simply to kill and destroy, made to strike terror into human hearts for the sake of human power and empire. Who is to say that such machines do not ultimately come . . . from the bottomless pit, under the direction of Apollyon?[3]

Do the locusts of Revelation lay behind modern warfare, or is their work evident in the torment of despair and isolation that people experience in an insecure world? Will the locusts be visible or are they spiritual demons seen only by John? We cannot be dogmatic. Perhaps Wright was correct to associate modern war machines with Apollyon. Conversely, the locusts may reflect the spiritual agony that accompanies a life without God. Either way, the worldview of Scripture assumes the existence of demonic forces that seek to direct our focus away from God even as God and his prophets remind us that we are not in control and must return to him.

One final point about how the locusts differ from the preceding trumpet blasts bears mentioning: God's people have no need to fear the demons of the fifth trumpet. The terror inflicted by the locusts is not transferrable to those whose hope is in Jesus. Although Christians may suffer, we do not fear because we know the Lamb is on the throne and we know that our suffering is evidence of our union with Jesus (Rom 8:17; Phil 3:10–11; James 1:2–3; 1 Pet 4:12–13). The fear aroused by the demon-locusts comes when people recognize that they have no protection. Idolatry and human self-sufficiency offer no solace in the storm and leave torture devoid of meaning. It is no wonder people sought death (Rev 9:6). Still, in God's mercy, death eluded the people, providing time to repent. In the sounding of the fifth trumpet, sin is revealed, sovereignty is challenged, and the world is upheaved. One woe is past. Behold! Two more remain.

---

3. Wright, *Revelation for Everyone*, 87.

The Sixth Trumpet

Following the anguish inflicted by the demon-locusts, the sixth trumpet heralds a demon-cavalry that annihilates one third of humanity; one out of every three people—gone.

When the trumpet sounded, an unidentified voice from the altar commanded the loosing of four angels from the Euphrates River (Rev 9:14). The four angels share their identity with the two hundred million strong cavalry (v. 16). As we saw in chapter 2, apocalyptic literature can symbolize one reality in multiple ways. What links the cavalry and the angels is an important repetition: both slay one-third of humanity (Rev 9:15, 18). Other numbers also commend this reading. The number four represents completeness. Thus, the four angels bring the full brunt of the trumpets to bear on sinful humanity.

The number "two hundred million" is a translator's best guess at how to render the Greek in v. 16. A literal translation of the Greek is "double-myriads of myriads." The word *myrias* means ten thousand when preceded by a numeric adjective (e.g., two), but what does "double-myriads of myriads" mean? What is twenty thousands of ten thousands and what did John mean when he said, "I heard their number?"

The exact number is less important than the overall picture: John is describing an incomprehensibly large army of the sort one sees in modern fantasy movies such as Peter Jackson's rendering of Tolkien's *Return of the King*, or the MCU's *Avengers: Endgame*. The point is not to do a head count of the army. Rather, it is in the grim detail that this horde of mind-boggling size obliterates one-third of the planet's population. One of every three people is gone.

For John's readers, the description of the horsemen, and their origin at the Euphrates River, recalled the Parthian Empire. We do not often think of Romans being afraid of military invasion, but Romans feared the Parthians—who were skilled archers mounted on horses that could shoot both backwards and forwards.

As with the locusts, it is difficult to say what reality, or even what kind of reality, John had in mind when he described these creatures. Is he speaking about a future battle between earthly armies? Do these fearsome horsemen symbolize the onslaught of demons released to slaughter one-third of humanity? Or, as one interpreter suggested, does their origin from the Euphrates and the power found in the mouths of the horses suggest that the sixth trumpet envisions the same event as the sixth bowl (Rev 16:12–16)?[4] This association would mean these creatures are actually deceiving spirits that lead people astray into not only physical but also spiritual death prior to the final judgement, or perhaps as part of the final judgment.[5]

It is easy to get lost in the details. The bottom line is we cannot be certain. Was John describing a future battle? Perhaps. Does he mean physical or spiritual death, or both? Perhaps. Does the sixth trumpet call prophetically to the church of John's time and our own? Absolutely! It reminds readers of our need to follow the Lamb, regardless of what the horsemen do. Even if believers find themselves among the one-third of humanity that is killed by this cavalry, the church does not need to fear because of Calvary. The Lamb that died has purchased her redemption and the trumpet calls to Jesus those with ears to hear.

6. Hard Hearts and Idolatry (Revelation 9:20–21)

The rapid succession of the first six trumpets ushered in one catastrophe after another. As Revelation placed creation under the microscope, readers find that the problem of sin runs deep ... very deep. It is not only humanity that falls under God's judgment. Sin has metastasized to the land, the sea, and the heavens. Virtually all creation endures hardship of one form or another. With the fifth and sixth trumpets, we also learn that it is not simply a natural order problem; the supernatural world is involved too. Demon-locusts and the four angels from the Euphrates run rampant killing up to a third of humanity and torturing those unprotected by God's seal.

All of this raises the question: what's the point? Are the trumpets (and the seals and bowls, for that matter) a divine temper tantrum from a deity fed up with sin? That question probably misrepresents God's justice, but it also misses the New Testament's conviction that God's ultimate answer to sin is to conquer it in the death and resurrection of the incarnate Son. The Lamb who sits on the throne is core to God's identity in Revelation and that identity ought not to be separated from our reflection on the trumpets.

So what is the role of the trumpet judgments? Revelation 9:20–21 hints at an answer. The plagues had a twofold purpose: to identify sin and to offer time for repentance. Depending on our frame of reference, we experience this action as the height of God's mercy and grace, or as the harshness

4. Beale, *Book of Revelation*, 513.
5. Beale, *Book of Revelation*, 515.

of the wrath of the Lamb (cf. Rev 6:17), even though the language of wrath is unused in Rev 8–9.

Given the many parallels to Exodus in this section of Revelation, consideration of the purpose behind the plagues in Exodus may be instructive for us. In Exodus, the plagues demonstrated God's sovereignty, which was in conflict with Pharaoh's claims to power. In the plagues, God demonstrated that God had the upper hand and in the process he also hardened Pharaoh's heart (Exod 4:21; 7:3).

Gregory Beale observes that the point of the Egyptian plagues—as that of the trumpets—was to glorify God. They were judgments because God not only foreknew Pharaoh's hard heart, he also caused it.[6] Many modern Christians would—and should—have theological and ethical problems with Beale's superficial reading of Exodus, which also misdirects his interpretation of the trumpets in Revelation.

A close reading of Exodus tempers the hardening of Pharaoh's heart. In the power struggle between Pharaoh and God, the former also hardens his own heart (Exod 8:15, 32). In fact, at the very beginning of the clash of sovereignties, Pharaoh's heart was already in a hardened condition (Exod 7:13). Old Testament scholar Victor Hamilton observed that it is not until the sixth plague that God actually hardened Pharaoh's heart.[7] God had given Pharaoh ample time to recognize this hardness of heart and admit his true powerlessness, but Pharaoh refused. In return, God did what Paul spoke about in Rom 1:24–25: he handed Pharaoh over to his sinful desires, which causes a hardness of heart. In this sense, God did indeed harden Pharaoh's heart, but it was in response to Pharaoh's refusal to repent.

What does all this have to do with Revelation? For starters, Beale was correct to identify the similar purpose between the trumpets and plagues. His problem was a superficial reading of Exodus. The plagues were opportunities for the empire to repent as God called his people out from under its power. The same is true in Revelation: God calls his people into the kingdom of God. This creates a clash of sovereignties that Douglas Webster explained well:

> The Egyptian plagues were designed "to systematically demolish every god-illusion or god-pretension that evil uses to exercise power over men and women." The trumpet blasts in Revelation

---

6. Beale and Campbell, *Revelation: A Shorter Commentary*, 171; cf. Beale, *Book of Revelation*, 465.

7. Hamilton, *Exodus: An Exegetical Commentary*, 145.

fulfill that same purpose. They herald the sovereignty of God against biological determinism, philosophical materialism, and metaphysical naturalism. Nature does not rule—God rules.[8]

Revelation 9:20–21 makes explicit that the core problem relates to a central theme of Revelation: worship. Who is worshiped? People have refused to surrender their worship of idols and demons and the sinful practices that go along with them. This has created a power struggle between God and our world because God seeks to redeem a people from the world of Pharaoh (and from Pharaoh's modern reincarnations). The trumpets have placed that world and its sin under the microscope and the full extent of idolatry has come into focus. They reveal how desperate our situation is, how impotent our idols—and we ourselves—are, and how badly we need Christ.

That call to repentance, however, will appear only as punishment for those who abhor the idea of following the Lamb and living like him. Because God does not force anyone into his kingdom, these people have a choice whether or not to repent. For the people of Rev 9:20–21, the lure of idolatry was so appealing that they chose not to leave the false power of idols behind. As with Jezebel and her followers in Rev 2:21–23, Jesus offered time to repent but they had no desire to do so. It is painful to leave the embrace of our idols, but remaining there hardens the human heart.

7. Conclusion

In the sounding of the trumpets, we hear horrifying calls to repentance. Sin, when it is closely examined, is scary. Even scarier is the response of humanity once sin is identified: *we don't want to let it go*. The fearsome part of the trumpets is not really bitter water, demon locusts, or even mass death. What should terrify us is that many will remain deaf to the trumpet calls to follow the Lamb. The scary part about sin is its allure that holds us captive and the harder we cling to it, the more recalcitrant our heart becomes against to the wooing of the Holy Spirit.

Let those with ears to hear, heed the sounding of the trumpets, repent, and live a life patterned after the Lamb.

---

8. Webster, *Follow the Lamb*, 157.

For Further Study

Discussion Questions

1. Where can you see God's mercy in Rev 8–9?

2. Many of the verbs associated with demons in Rev 9 are in the passive voice: the angel in v. 1 *is given* a key, he does not take it. The locusts *are given* authority (v. 5), they do not act on their own accord. The four angels in v. 15 *are let lose* to go and slaughter, they do not free themselves. What does this suggest about who is in control? How might it challenge our view of God in a sort of real contest with Satan?

3. What might be an idol in your life that, if God challenged its power, you would see it as punishment rather than a call to repentance?

For Further Reading

- Bauckham, Richard. *The Theology of the Book of Revelation*. Cambridge: Cambridge University Press, 1993, 80–84.

- Webster, Douglas. *Follow the Lamb: A Pastoral Approach to Revelation*. Eugene: Cascade Books, 2014, 154–64.

- Wright, N. T. *Revelation for Everyone*. Louisville: Westminster John Knox, 2011, 84–92.

8

Anticipating the Kingdom's Arrival

Preparatory reading:

- Revelation 10–11
- Ezekiel 2:1—3:3

1. Introduction

In high school, I played soccer and—decades after the fact—I still remember well those practices the coach devoted to the team's physical fitness. My favorite part of practice on those days was the water break. After the agonizing time spent running around the soccer field, my lungs gasped for air and my mouth cried out for water. If the coach happened to be in a bad mood on those days, we simply hoped not to provoke him, which would assuredly incur additional punishment being exacted from our already tired muscles. Break time was sweet relief.

That relief is almost how Rev 10–11 feels. After two chapters of jumping from one catastrophe to another, readers long for it to be over. Revelation 9 concluded with an evil cavalry that annihilated a third of humanity. Even then, humanity remained obdurate in its refusal to repent. Now, in Rev 10, John sees something new. Just as Rev 7 interrupted the seal judgments, Rev 10:1—11:14 interrupts the progression from the sixth to seventh trumpets.

2. John's Prophetic Call (Revelation 10:1–11)

After the stampede of destruction heralded by the sixth trumpet, John saw a mighty angel who descended and stood with one foot on the land and one on the sea. Several biblical images layer the description of the angel. The rainbow over his head recalls the one surrounding the throne in Rev 4:3, as well as the rainbow surrounding God in Ezek 1:28. The face that shines like the sun echoes the description of Jesus (Rev 1:16), as might his association with a cloud (Rev 14:14; cf. Exod 14:24; Dan 7:13). Additionally, the combination of the cloud imagery with legs like a pillar of fire reminds readers of the Exodus themes that were prevalent in the first six trumpet judgments (Exod 13:21–22). Finally, the command to seal up what the prophet witnessed closely resembles the angel's instruction in Dan 12:4.

In Rev 10, the angel's identity is a bit of a conundrum. It is impossible to determine whether the angel is Jesus, a graphic symbol of God's presence drawing on several Old Testament texts, or some high-ranking member of the heavenly court. What is clear is that this figure operates with God's authority in one way or another. He holds a scroll that contains words from God that John must transmit to his readers.

Understanding the Scroll

Scholars of Revelation cannot agree whether this is the same scroll that had seven seals in Rev 5. Perhaps it—like the one in Rev 5—does contain the mystery of God's plan for bringing ultimate salvation. If so, it would also likely contain judgments, which is why some believe the events of Rev 11:1–13 reveal the scroll's contents. Perhaps. We cannot say for certain.

More important to John was scroll's role within the heavenly scene of Rev 10. Significantly, that scene resembles prophetic commissioning stories from the Old Testament. Consider the similarities to Ezekiel's commissioning in Ezek 2:

Table 2
Similarities Between the Scrolls of Revelation 10 and Ezekiel 2

	Ezekiel 2:1–3:3	Revelation 10:8–10
The prophet is sent to speak	2:3–5	10:11
Command to eat a scroll	2:8—3:1	10:8–9
Report that the prophet ate the scroll	3:2	10:10
Report on the sweet taste of the scroll in the prophet's mouth	3:3	10:10

As with any prophetic commission, John was called to announce God's plan as God revealed it to him. The revelation of that plan is what v. 7 had in view when it spoke about God's mystery being completed (or accomplished) in the days preceding the seventh trumpet. The angel at the beginning of Rev 10 connected that mystery with the gospel by clarifying that it was "proclaimed as good news" to (and through) the prophets (Rev 10:7). Many English translations say that the mystery of God was "announced" to the prophets, which is an adequate translation. However, it obscures a double entendre in Greek, which employs the word for announcing specifically good news—it is the same root behind "evangelize" and "gospel" in English. This obfuscation is regrettable since John likely has the gospel in mind in v. 7.

The prophetic proclamation of the gospel that John received tasted sweet, but also stimulated bitterness within him. Salvation is a sweet gift. The message that the Lamb is on the throne and that the Good Shepherd has come to lead his people is a comforting and delicious message to digest. But the gospel message is a sweet-and-sour one because it contains both salvation and judgment. The gospel also has a bitter side: God does not force people into his kingdom and those who choose to rebel face the king's wrath. This is the same point Jesus made in the parable of the tenants in Luke 20:9–18.

That parable might also bring to mind an additional aspect of the bitter aftertaste of John's commission: many who hear the prophetic proclamation fail to receive it well. In Jesus' parable, the emissaries sent by the father were beaten or killed. Likewise, John had already suffered persecution and found himself exiled on Patmos. Part of a prophet's bitterness is the frustration of addressing people with closed ears (Isaiah) and rebellious characters (Ezekiel). John's own experience of this bitterness is reported in Rev 10:10 and is echoed in the trials of the church in chapter 11.

Tick, Tock, Tick, Tock

One concept that lingers in the background of Rev 10 is that the time to repent is short and will soon elapse (10:6). That may well be the meaning behind the sealing of the seven thunders in vv. 3–4. Most interpreters suspect the thunders revealed another set of judgments God planned to unleash. However, in light of the ineffectiveness of the judgments at rooting out sin and securing repentance (Rev 2:21; 9:20–21; cf. 16:9, 11), God chose to short-circuit these and bring about his final judgment (the seventh trumpet). This is consistent with Jesus' statement in Mark 13:20 about the days before his return being cut short.

Time to hear the gospel, repent, and follow the Lamb is expiring quickly. In Rev 10, John once again receives his commission to preach this prophetic message. But who will hear it and how will they respond? That is the question that chapter eleven will address in the verses that follow.

3. Picturing the Church (Revelation 11:1–10)

Revelation 11 provides several pictures of the people who received John's prophetic message—the church. We encounter this people as Rev 11:1–13 reports a vision that some interpreters believe summarized or portrayed the message John was commissioned to preach in Rev 10. The vision breaks into two sections. Verses 1–2 focus on the measuring of the temple and vv. 3–13 contain John's description of the ministry of two witnesses.

Measuring the Temple (Revelation 11:1–2)

The Greek vocabulary and grammar of Rev 11:1–2 are not particularly complex, which makes translating the words fairly straightforward. John received a reed and was instructed to measure the temple, omitting its outer precinct because it would be given over to the gentiles. Even so, despite the untechnical language, determining the meaning of these verses sharply divides scholars.

The Romans had destroyed the Jerusalem temple in 70 CE, leaving it as only a memory when John penned Revelation some twenty (or more) years later. Nevertheless, the temple was the setting for John's vision. The temple as John had known it divided into several courts. The inner court, called the Court of the Priests, contained the altar where priests officiated worship services and sacrifices. The outer courtyard, called the Court of the Gentiles, was where God-fearing non-Jews were permitted to worship. It was this courtyard that John omitted from his measurements. That much we understand, but what does it mean?

Gregory Beale identified no less than five distinct ways interpreters have understood these verses.[1] Three of these are:

- Dispensational futurists believe Rev 11:1–2 predicts a rebuilt Jerusalem temple preceding Christ's return. The distinction between its measured and unmeasured precincts symbolizes believing ethnic Jews and non-believing ethnic Jews. The former—those who are measured—enjoy physical protection from God at some future point when the gentiles will overrun the temple.

- Another view concludes that the temple symbolizes the church. As such, its measured portions depict Christians under God's protection and preserved for salvation. By contrast, the unmeasured parts of the temple represent unfaithful Christians who have compromised the gospel and forfeited God's spiritual protection (e.g., the followers of Balaam and Jezebel in Rev 2–3).

- Finally, many interpreters believe Rev 11:1–2 depicts the same reality—the church—from two different angles. From one angle, the church is measured for protection by God and kept safe in his presence. On the other hand, the church also exists in a hostile world where it gets trampled; it is susceptible to persecution.

Despite their differences, these approaches do exhibit a degree of commonality. Each interpretation reads the text symbolically (including the dispensationalists, who typically advertise their approach as "literal"). For instance, virtually everyone agrees the act of measuring represents divine protection (whether physical or spiritual). This conclusion is supported by Zech 2:1–5 , which many interpreters identify as a source for Revelation's imagery. In Zechariah, God's protection immediately follows the measuring of the temple.

One can make intelligent arguments in favor of each of the views we have considered. Significantly, though, each of them also has difficulties. For the dispensational futurist, it is difficult get beyond John's ecclesiology (his doctrine of God's people), which drives no wedge between Jewish

---

1. Beale and Campbell, *Revelation: A Shorter Commentary*, 214–15.

and non-Jewish believers. Also problematic is the lack of any distinction in Revelation between believing ethnic Jews and non-believing ethnic Jews. Ethnic Judaism does not appear to be on John's radar. Even if it was, the apparent resumption of the sacrificial system poses a major theological hurdle for the dispensational reading. Hebrews 9:11–28 made clear that Jesus' sacrifice as our high priest was once for all; there is no longer a need to sacrifice. Consequently, any resumption of the temple and sacrificial system would, by definition, involve those rejecting the Messiah's fulfillment of the sacrificial system. Even if these were ethnic Jews, does Revelation ever offer hope to those who have rejected the Lamb?

The latter two options fair much better. The notion that the measured portion of the temple symbolizes the faithful who experience spiritual protection is appealing. In this sense, the measuring resembles that of the sealing of the 144,000—it is not a physical protection, but a spiritual preservation of those who remain faithful.

Both interpretations also make good points regarding the temple's unmeasured—or unprotected—portions. This could symbolize people who fall away from the faith. These forfeit their spiritual protection and fall under God's judgment. As in Rom 1:26–32, God's judgment of sin allows it to have its full effect on people who persist in rejecting God. This situation could well be the condition symbolized by the trampling of the city in Rev 11:2.

Conversely, the unmeasured parts of the temple might portray the church in its engagement with the world. This would exemplify Revelation's penchant for depicting one reality from multiple angles. Whereas the faithful enjoy spiritual protection, they also experience pain and persecution. Physically, followers of the (slaughtered) Lamb endure victimization by powers of evil just as Jesus did. Like the unmeasured temple and the holy city, it appears they are without protection. Spiritually, however, this struggling people is protected (measured) by God. The powers of evil will find themselves unable to touch the church's "real source of life."[2]

The Two Witnesses (Revelation 11:3–14)

The unnamed voice that instructed John to measure the temple also mentioned the prophetic ministry of the church, symbolized by two witnesses who struggle with the beast.

---

2. Mounce, *Revelation*, 214.

In Rev 1:13, 20, lampstands symbolized the church. Consequently, the association of the two witnesses with "the two lampstands that are before the Lord" in Rev 11:4 points to their symbolic identity. Verse 4 also employed the metaphor of olive trees, likely echoing Zech 4, where the prophet saw two olive trees on either side of a lampstand. An angel told Zechariah the trees represented two anointed ones standing beside the Lord of all the earth (Zech 4:14). Most interpreters of Zechariah believe his prophecy pertained to the roles of Joshua (the high priest) and Zerubbabel (the Persian governor) during his own time.

Revelation 11 repurposed Zechariah's imagery. The trees still represent the anointed ones who stand before the Lord, but their symbolic representation as lampstands expands their identities beyond two individuals to include the prophetic ministry of the church. This ministry is carried out with sackcloth—the garb of mourning and repentance (Rev 11:3). The witnesses have tasted the bitterness of the scroll John ate in Rev 10:10 and call the world to repentance and to mourn sinfulness.

Having said this, there is an inherent weakness to interpretations that identify the two witnesses with the church. Their ability to spew fire and kill their enemies is very much at odds with the depiction of the church elsewhere in Revelation. At first glance, such "victory" does not resemble the Lamb. This could suggest the witnesses do not symbolize the church and are in fact two individuals. Many have adopted that view, but it also has difficulties. Gregory Beale summarizes some of these well:[3]

- The war waged against the witnesses by the beast in v. 7 seemingly alludes to Dan 7:21 in which the community of saints—not two individuals—is attacked.

- The ability of the whole world to see the destruction of the two witnesses in vv. 9–13 makes sense if they symbolize a worldwide church; the notion that John saw modern technology and media broadcasting of two dead bodies seems less convincing.

- The length of the prophecy of the two witnesses (1,260 days) corresponds to the forty-two months that the holy city is trampled in v. 2, which likely envisions the church. Also, it is the same length of time the woman in Rev 12:6—who also symbolizes the church—must find refuge in the wilderness.

---

3. Beale and Campbell, *Revelation: A Shorter Commentary*, 220–21.

- The act of witnessing, or testifying, that defines the two people in Rev 11:3–13 is the hallmark of the church's activity elsewhere in Revelation (6:9; 12:11; 19:10; 20:4)

Given these considerations, understanding the two witnesses as a symbol for the church remains the preferable option. But what about the discrepancy created between their fiery spittle and Revelation's portrayal of the church elsewhere? That question requires us to consider the witnesses's task within the story that Revelation is telling. To ask about the fire from their mouths is to ask about their witness, which emanates from the same source.

1. The Witnesses' Prophetic Ministry

To begin, we should recognize that if the two witnesses themselves are symbolic, so is the fire of their mouths. The second-century Jewish apocalyptic work 4 Ezra employed similar symbolism to describe the Messiah's judgment of the nations (4 Ezra 13:1–12, 21–38). In that book, the Messiah did not conquer with conventional weapons, but spewed fire from his mouth. In 4 Ezra's story, God interpreted the vision, explaining that the fire symbolized conquering the nations through the law (4 Ezra 13:38), meaning the Torah (God's instruction in the Old Testament), which certainly contained judgments for sin.

That kind of symbolism resembles Rev 11:5. The two witnesses do not lash out in vengeance toward all who oppose them. Rather, they prophesy (Rev 11:3, 6); they speak the words of God (cf. Jer 5:14). Such words—the gospel of Jesus—do indeed torment those who would rather not hear from God (see 1 Kgs 22:8). Similarly, people often perceive the message proclaimed by Christians today as judgmental and for that reason sometimes oppose the church. The response of the faithful to persecution, however, is not to destroy the persecutors. Rather, the church's work is to bear witness to the resurrection and Jesus' identity as the Messiah. That witness itself torments those who enjoy sin. This is how the church claims victory: not through use of weapons (or anything resembling literal fire), but through the word of our testimony that constitutes a fiery call to repentance.

Two individuals foreshadow this prophetic ministry of the church: Moses and Elijah, the two archetypal prophets from the Old Testament. Like Moses, the two witnesses in Rev 11 called down plagues and turned water into blood (Exod 7:14–12:30). Like Elijah, they shut up the sky to prevent rain (1 Kgs 17–18).

But why these particular men? Why symbolize the church as Moses and Elijah? In ancient Judaism—within which John was steeped—there was an expectation that Moses and Elijah would appear in the last days (see Deut 18:15; Mal 4:5). Drawing from this tradition, Moses and Elijah embody in Revelation the bittersweet prophetic message that John and the church proclaim. Moses recalled the story of Exodus and his role in leading people out of Egypt; Elijah's ministry included a staunch stand against idolatry on Mt. Carmel and the killing of Baal's prophets after that event. Likewise, the church calls people out of sin and into God's kingdom by proclaiming the message of liberation from sin and idolatry.

2. The Witnesses' War with the Beast

The task of proclaiming the church's call to repentance is accomplished in a world filled with beasts. This is why the spiritual protection afforded to the faithful in Rev 11:1–2 is so important. Even as God's people are trampled by the world, God empowers them to fulfill their role as prophets. Once that prophecy is complete, the beast appears in full force to make war against them.

The beast from the abyss makes his first appearance in Revelation 11:7. He is likely the beast from the sea or the dragon we will encounter in later chapters. Regardless, it remains clear from the outset that he opposes God's people and will gain the upper hand, claiming victory through killing the witnesses (Rev 11:7–8). Bearing witness to Jesus' lordship and calling out the idolatry of those who rebel against his lordship incurs the world's wrath.

John saw the witnesses martyred in a city that is a spiritual Sodom and Egypt (Rev 11:8). Jerusalem is the city John has in mind. However, if the witnesses symbolize the worldwide church, it seems probable that the city in view symbolizes a larger reality than Jerusalem alone (some commentators associate it with the Roman Empire). The point behind the city in which the witnesses are martyred is that it stands in place of a world opposed to the Messiah who brings God's righteousness. Just as the world killed the Messiah, it also kills his witnesses.

With the martyring of the witnesses, John did not intend to say every Christian would die. Rather, the point is that the church—like the crucified

Jesus—will appear defeated. The beast will have victory and the world will rejoice.

Martyrdom, however, is not the end of the story. A resurrection is coming. As with Jesus, the resurrection is the moment of vindication for the body of Christ. In the resurrection, the truth of the church's testimony becomes evident and the faithful are called to ascend to heaven as Jesus did (and as John was summoned in Rev 4:1).

Some believe this anticipates a physical rapture of the church. In fact, this is probably the closest Revelation comes to saying anything akin to the rapture as it is popularly conceived. If that is what we have here, it is also important to recognize that it immediately precedes a worldwide glorification of God (Rev 11:13), the sounding of the seventh trumpet (v. 15), and the arrival of God's kingdom (vv. 15-19).

Others prefer a more symbolic reading of the resurrection scene in Rev 11:11-12. The difficulty in this case, however, is identifying precisely the reality being symbolized. Perhaps the ascension language points to some means of Jesus vindicating his church as true prophets, but the means of that vindication remain unclear.

Regardless of whether one opts for a physical ascension or a symbolic interpretation, the implication for the church and the world remains the same: God will vindicate the church as his true witnesses and the world will fear and subsequently glorify God (Rev 11:13).

Simultaneous with the church's vindication, an earthquake destroyed a tenth of the city and killed seven thousand people. That event echoes other biblical passages about God coming in judgment. This time, however, the judgment effects a different result.

As we have seen, the judgments in Revelation have thus far yielded no results in producing repentance. However, following the witness, suffering, and vindication of the church, those who remain give glory to God (Rev 11:13). This is the victorious end of the war with the beast: God is glorified and creation recognizes the church's witness about Jesus as true. The time has come for God's kingdom to be established!

4. The Seventh Trumpet (Revelation 11:15-19)

With the sounding of the trumpet, God's final victory appears. A great voice called out the memorable words from Handel's "Hallelujah Chorus":

"The kingdom of this world is become the kingdom of our Lord, and of His Christ."[4]

N. T. Wright correctly observed that the domain of God's rule in Revelation is far greater than what we find in popular theologies about the end times.[5] Typically, western Christians imagine God reigning in heaven and possess the hope of one day departing this world to dwell with him there. Revelation 11:15 paints a quite different picture. The God who created the universe does not surrender it to evil and chaos. Rather, the rebellious kingdom of our world *becomes* God's kingdom and the sounding of the seventh trumpet heralds the arrival of God's reign on earth.

The twenty-four elders responded to the annunciation of God's kingdom by falling prostrate and resuming their unending heavenly worship. Their praise of "the one who is and who was" echoes statements made by the four living creatures and Jesus himself (Rev 11:17; cf. 1:8; 4:8), but there is an important difference. Jesus identified himself as "the one who is and who was and who is to come" (1:8). In Rev 11:17, the elders worship the one who is and who was; God is no longer the one who is coming. Rather, he has come.

This strongly suggests Revelation associates the seventh trumpet with the final judgment and arrival of God. As we saw in our study of the trumpets (chapter 7), Revelation is not written in a linear fashion with everything building up to the bowl judgments. Instead, it depicts God's victory from a series of angles and the seventh trumpet is the culmination of one of those vantage points.

In the seventh trumpet, the elders praised God for beginning to reign. The nations were enraged, but God's wrath came (note that the word "wrath" in Rev 11:18 typically envisages God's final judgment in Revelation; see Rev 14:10–11; 16:19; 19:15). The time arrived to judge the dead and reward the faithful. Regarding the latter, v. 18 offers three pictures of the church: they are God's servants, the prophets; the saints; and those who fear God's name. They are the ones who received the sweetness of the message proclaimed in the scroll John ate in Rev 10:10.

Even so, the last line of Rev 11:18 recalls the bitterness of that message. The time arrived not only for rewarding the faithful, but for "destroying the destroyers of the earth" (author's translation). The trumpet judgments

---

4 Handel, "Hallelujah Chorus."

5. Wright, *Revelation for Everyone*, 102–4.

placed sin and its destruction under the microscope and with the seventh trumpet God completed the spiritual surgery that removed them.

Once God removed sin, the heavenly temple opened and revealed the ark of the covenant. In the Old Testament, the ark was God's footstool in the holy of holies. It was so closely associated with God's presence that Philistines mistook it for an idol of Israel's deity (1 Sam 4:5–7). Likewise, in Rev 11:19, the ark symbolizes God's presence. With the sounding of the final trumpet, that presence is no longer contained in heaven's inner sanctum. Instead, John saw God's kingdom envelop the world. God arrived in victory and the whole of creation received access to God's presence as it reverberated with thunder and earthquakes, flashes of lightning, and a great hailstorm.

5. Prophecy in Revelation 10–11

Before concluding our exploration of Rev 10–11, we must consider the theme of prophecy. The word group that includes prophecy, prophet, prophesy, etc. is highly concentrated in these chapters. The only other place this word group occurs with such frequency in Revelation is its final chapter.

The high concentration of the terminology here shows that prophecy is the theme that unites Rev 10–11. As such, prophecy must represent an important characteristic of the church (the main subject of Rev 11) and its message (the main subject of Rev 10).

Revelation 10:7 introduced the theme of prophecy by representing the church as a prophetic community during the days preceding the seventh trumpet. As part of that community, John received the commission to prophesy concerning peoples, nations, languages, and kings (Rev 10:11). Significantly, the terms for peoples and nations in John's audience reemerge in 11:9 as those who rejoiced over the cessation and apparent defeat of the prophetic witness of the church (11:9–10). Then, with the sounding of the final trumpet, the twenty-four elders describe the church, again, as God's prophets (11:18).

It is worth reiterating that biblical prophecy is not first and foremost about predicting the future. When Rev 10–11 fixates on the church's prophetic ministry, it is not a summons for Christians to begin prognosticating regarding stock market crashes, one world governments, etc. Rather, it is a reminder that our role is to proclaim God's message—the gospel—to a world in need of salvation.

As with John's scroll, that gospel message will taste both bitter and sweet. On the one hand, some will savor the sweetness of salvation because of the church's testimony about Jesus. Conversely, a bitter aftertaste follows the gospel when we realize that Jesus is Lord and does not share sovereignty with the kingdom of this world. That kingdom is being supplanted by Christ's kingdom and those who refuse his rule will ultimately fall under his judgment when sin is removed.

Revelation 10–11 reminds the church that our task is to bear faithful witness to Jesus' true identity. That is a prophetic ministry that summons the kingdom of this world to repentance. The prophetic message torments those who prefer not to hear the gospel. Because of that torment, Christians expect resistance and opposition. Nevertheless, like the two witnesses, Christians do not claim victory through conquering their persecutors. Rather, our victory is in Christlikeness. Victory comes through apparent defeat and sometimes martyrdom because that is what a faithful representation of Jesus looks like.

For those of us who are at home in comfortable churches like those in Laodicea and Sardis, or who have been led astray by false teachings like the churches of Pergamum and Thyatira, Rev 10–11 becomes a wake-up call. Faithfulness and faithful witnessing are decidedly uncomfortable and entail the awkward ministry and hardships of prophets who resolutely proclaim, "Thus says the Lord..." to a world with closed ears. By contrast, to suffering Christians in places like Smyrna and Philadelphia, Rev 10–11 reminds us that victory comes through the witness we proclaim. We may lose friends and family because of faithfulness to Christ, but our union with him in his death and his resurrection will result in vindication and the conversion of those who see the church's final victory (Rev 11:13).

6. Conclusion

Revelation 10–11 narrates the final days, when the church's proclamation of the gospel will reach its completion. That proclamation happens over a limited period of time (forty-two months in Rev 11:2; 1,260 days in 11:3; three and a half years in 11:7). Put differently, the prophetic ministry of the church is not an eternal ministry. Rather, the church testifies about the Lamb for a set period of time and the time is coming quickly when the final trumpet will sound and the ministry will complete. When that happens, we will be caught up in the worship of the twenty-four elders as we praise the one who is and who was because he has taken his great power and begun to reign (11:17). The kingdom of this world will become the kingdom of our Lord and of his Messiah.

For Further Study

Discussion Questions

1. How does the prophetic aspect of the church's mission impact your understanding of your role as a witness to who Jesus is?
2. Regardless of whether the two witnesses of Rev 11 are literal individuals or symbolize the church, what might their willingness to undergo martyrdom communicate to us about how Christians live here and now?
3. Which church from Rev 2–3 best reflects your faith community and how does that venue impact what we should take away from Rev 10–11?

For Further Reading

- Wright, N. T. *Revelation for Everyone*. Louisville: Westminster John Knox, 2011, 92–106.

9

Worship Wars

Preparatory reading:

- Revelation 12–14
- Daniel 7

1. Introduction

During my first semester in college, I found myself enrolled in a British literature course. As someone whose prior exposure to British literature and theater was limited to Monty Python's depiction of King Arthur and cartoon versions of Robin Hood, I was quite lost. Especially difficult for me were works by Jonathan Swift such as *Gulliver's Travels*, which employed symbolism to depict political problems in eighteenth-century Europe. My historical and cultural distance from Swift meant that the symbols he employed conveyed no meaning to me. When Swift wrote about conflicts between the Lilliputians and Blefuscudians, it never occurred to me that England and France were in the background.

Similarly, Rev 12–14 retells the story of Jesus and God's people with such extensive symbolism that modern readers can fail to recognize the true characters. As we have seen elsewhere, the imagery of the Old Testament saturates Revelation. Consequently, readers unfamiliar with the Old Testament (and apocalyptic literature) experience difficulty when reading Rev 12–14, just as I struggled to understand Swift's writing. Thankfully, though, our study of apocalyptic literature and Revelation up to this point has prepared us to hear the story John tells.

2. A Woman, a Child, and a Dragon (Revelation 12:1–6)

On the heels of the seventh trumpet, Rev 12 launches a new series of visions that lead into the seven bowl judgments (Rev 16). The initial vision in this series is a graphic representation of the birth and resurrection of Jesus.

The Woman

It began with a great sign: the appearance of a woman—clothed with the sun, the moon under her feet, and wearing a crown of twelve stars (Rev 12:1). She was pregnant and about to give birth. Her description reflects several biblical images. First and foremost, her birthing of a male child about to be gobbled up by a monster graphically recalls Mary and the imperiled early life of Jesus (see Matt 2:13–18).

But the woman is also larger than Mary. She symbolizes God's people—both before and after the earthly ministry of Jesus. The twelve stars, the sun, and the moon recall Joseph's dream in which these bodies symbolized the faithful covenant community (Jacob and his offspring; see Gen 37:9–10). Likewise, in Rev 12, those bodies signify the woman's identity as God's people. Elsewhere, the Old Testament depicted Israel as a woman in pain of childbirth to represent the difficulties and persecutions experienced by God's people (Isa 26:17; cf. 66:7–11). So also, the woman of Rev 12 was pained as God's people awaited the Messiah, who would be born in their midst.

Once the child—Jesus—ascended, the dragon forced the woman into hiding and warred against her children (Rev 12:13–17). Significantly, the woman's time in the wilderness—1,260 days (12:6, 14)—parallels the duration of the two witnesses' testimony (11:3). In fact, the woman and the witnesses are one and the same: God's people throughout the ages who worship and follow the Messiah, even while pursued by the dragon.

The woman's refuge in the wilderness deserves attention for a couple of reasons. First, it was prepared by God. Even in trials and persecution, God has provided spiritual protection for his people. Secondly, despite God's protection, the identification of the place as a wilderness suggests it was also less than ideal. Wilderness is not the final resting place for God's people. Rather, they inhabit it for a limited time: three and a half years. There are echoes here to Israel's time in the wilderness, which was likewise a time of testing and trial, but also the time when God supplied their needs through manna, quail, and water. Like Israel, Jesus' followers exist in a place that is less than ideal, but faithfulness to him leads to God's salvation and victory (Rev 12:10–11).[1]

The Child

The pains experienced by the woman gave way to the Messiah's birth and his ensuing escape from the dragon (Rev 12:2–5). Jesus was consumed neither by Herod's infanticide in Bethlehem nor by Pilate's brutality in Jerusalem. John communicates this message in two short sentences that move quickly from Jesus' birth to ascension. John says nothing about the earthly ministry of Jesus, but we know that Jesus is the child by the allusion to Ps 2 in Rev 12:5—a psalm that Jesus quoted of himself in Rev 2:27: "He will shepherd [the nations] with a rod of iron" (author's translation; cf. LXX Ps 2:9).

Speaking about the beginning and ending of Jesus' earthly life was a concise way to bring the entire story of Jesus into view. This is a literary way of doing what a toy pirate telescope does when it collapses into its compact form. Hebrew writers—like John—commonly alluded to an object by noting its extremities. For example, when the psalmist exclaimed that God is praised from the rising of the sun to the place where it sets, the implication was that God is praised everywhere, not only on the horizon. Similarly, Rev 12 summarized the gospel story by mentioning its starting point with Jesus' birth and its culmination with Jesus' vindication and ascension to the Father.

The Dragon

The conflict in this story stems from a second sign John witnessed—the dragon (Rev 12:3), which is one of the few symbols Revelation identifies explicitly (12:9). It is the devil and he was poised to consume the Messiah. He appears in menacing red hue with seven heads and ten crowns, symbolizing the totality of opposition to God's people. The swiping of a third

---

1. For additional parallels between Israel and the church's time in the wilderness, see Boeckel, "Saving Rest."

of the stars from the sky has multiple possible explanations. If Revelation is echoing a text like Dan 8:10, the stars could symbolize either angels or God's faithful people.

Many commentators believe the dragon's activities in Rev 12 drew upon well-known myths from the Roman world. While Roman readers might have perceived such connections, John more probably drew on biblical imagery for his writing. With that in mind, the dragon's characterization as an "ancient serpent" (Rev 12:9) recalls the multiheaded serpentine sea monster in the Old Testament—the leviathan (Ps 74:14; Isa 27:1; sometimes called "Rahab," see Ps 89:10; Isa 51:9). In the Septuagint (the Greek translation of the Old Testament), "leviathan" was often translated "dragon." Consequently, readers familiar with the Greek Old Testament who encountered the word "dragon" in Revelation would be at least as inclined to think about the leviathan as Roman mythology.

Even more specifically, the appearance of the dragon actually continues Revelation's use of the story of Exodus that we already observed in the trumpet judgments. This observation is confirmed by several Old Testament texts that connect that sea-monster dragon with the story of God's deliverance from Egypt (Isa 30:7; 51:9–10). Ezekiel even goes to the point of identifying the pharaoh of his time with the sea monster conquered by Israel's God (Ezek 29:3 LXX). If such comparisons hold in Rev 12, then the point is *not* that Egypt or Pharaoh were Satan-incarnate, but rather that their sinful behaviors assisted John in crafting the dragon's portrait.

3. A War and Worship (Revelation 12:7–18)

Sandwiched between the woman's introduction (Rev 12:1–6) and her wilderness experience (12:13–17) is a war and a song of victory in the last place one expects to find war: in heaven. What is going on here?

We begin by noting what these verses *do not* narrate: Rev 12:7–9 does not report a primordial battle between Satan and God. Revelation explains neither the origin of evil nor that of Satan. For that matter, the Bible never mentions a heavenly *coup d'état* waged by Satan in an attempt to overthrow God. Western Christians commonly imagine that kind of a cosmic combat as the devil's origin story, but Scripture remains silent on the matter. Much of our thinking on this is indebted to John Milton's *Paradise Lost* more than it is to Scripture.

What *is* Revelation describing, then? Revelation 12:7–9 tells the same story as vv. 1–6, but does so on a spiritual—or cosmic—level. Apocalyptic writings often contain heavenly counterparts to events and people that appear on earth. Revelation has already shown something similar with the churches in Rev 2–3, where each church had a corresponding angel in heaven. In Luke, Jesus himself acknowledged that the actions of his disciples had implications in heaven (Luke 10:17–20). Likewise, Michael appears in the apocalyptic sections of Daniel as a heavenly representative of God's people. In Rev 12:7–9, Michael's victory over the devil parallels Christ's victory (told in vv. 1–6).

The decisive victory, of course, occurred on earth at the cross. That is where God triumphed over evil. It is also why the song of victory in v. 11 says the followers of Jesus conquered the dragon by the blood of the Lamb (Rev 12:11). Jesus' sacrificial death is how God claimed victory. Michael's defeat of Satan represents a corresponding symbolic depiction of that spiritual battle in heaven. Just as death lacked the strength to hold Jesus, Satan lacked the strength to defeat Michael. George Caird summarized the relationship between Michael's victory in heaven and Jesus' victory on the cross:

> Michael's victory is simply the heavenly and symbolic counterpart of the earthly reality of the Cross. Michael, in fact, is not the field officer who does the actual fighting, but the staff officer in the heavenly control room, who is able to remove Satan's flag from the heavenly map because the real victory has been won on Calvary.[2]

The point of the graphic battle and the song of Rev 12:10–12 is that the death, resurrection, and ascension of Jesus vanquished the enemy and brought God's salvation. In Jesus' death, we find atonement for sin. In his resurrection and ascension, he conquered the wages of sin and was vindicated as Israel's Messiah who will rule the nations. This good news has hampered the dragon's ability to do what he does best: accuse.

In the Old Testament, Satan appeared as one accusing people of wrongdoing before God (Job 1:6–12; 2:1–6; Zech 3:1–2). In fact, the word *satan* is Hebrew for "accuser." That is the role Rev 12 alludes to in the song of victory (Rev 12:10). Satan's ability to accuse in the throne room of heaven is now removed because the faithful have claimed victory through the blood of the Lamb (12:11). When the blood of Jesus sanctifies a person

---

2. Caird, *Revelation of St. John*, 154.

from all unrighteousness, there is no longer any room for accusation before the Father. Jesus has taken the throne in heaven and the dragon is decisively cast out.

That is the heavenly picture. Meanwhile, on earth, the battle continues and the faithful become victorious not only through the blood of Jesus but also through their testimony (Rev 12:11). Through the church's testimony as it follows Jesus faithfully, the enemy is defeated on his own turf. Like Jesus' victory, ours may involve apparent defeat through suffering and death, but this is what faithfully following the Lamb often entails. It is how the dragon is defeated and because of this heaven rejoices.

The victory song of Rev 12:10–12 concludes with a warning to the earth and sea. The defeated dragon has been cast into this realm and like any wounded animal his anger rages, though his time is short. With the dragon's change of venue, the primary front of the war shifted from heaven to earth and the dragon resumed his persecution of the woman and her offspring. Earlier, we observed subtle parallels between the dragon and Egypt and that Exodus motif now continues. In Rev 12:14, God's people fled into the wilderness with wings resembling the portrayal of God's deliverance of Israel from Egypt (Exod 19:4). Additionally, any of John's readers familiar with Israel's crossing of the Red Sea can appreciate the parallel of the earth thwarting the dragon's pursuit of the woman by gulping down the threatening water, just as God provided dry land to overcome the threat posed by the Red Sea's waters (Exod 14).

Unable to touch the woman, the dragon departed to wage war with her children. It is here that we see the woman symbolized not only Israel but also the church—her offspring include those who keep God's commandments and who hold to the testimony of Jesus. These are the faithful who worship God and it is these with whom the beast will make war.

4. A Spiritual Proxy War (Revelation 13:1–18)

I had a bit of a mischievous side in my youth. I enjoyed pulling off practical jokes, but was typically too much of a "good kid" to do the dirty work myself. I was more suited to being the mastermind behind whatever mischief was transpiring; my deeds were accomplished by proxy. For instance, on a high school mission trip, while one of my best friends was in the shower, I orchestrated matters so that another friend decided it would be funny to hide the clothes of the one in the shower. Of course, it was that friend who got the blame and bore the brunt of the first friend's revenge . . . and I was snickering behind the scenes the whole time.

That is how the dragon operates in Rev 13. He is the mastermind behind the scenes and engages secondary parties to accomplish his evil designs.

The Beast from the Sea

The first instrument of the dragon appeared as the beast from the sea. Most commentators recognize the affinities between this beast and the ones in Dan 7. Whereas Daniel saw four beasts that symbolized different brutal empires, Rev 13 collapses those four into one beast that resembles each its predecessors (Rev 13:2; cf. Dan 7:3–8). The beast represents the totality of the evil of empire.

As in Daniel, this monster horrifies and acts with the authority and power of the dragon who now lurks behind the scenes. The beast also becomes a parody of Jesus. He possesses many of the characteristics attributed to the Lamb in Revelation:

- Both have horns (Rev 5:6; 13:3)
- Both appear to have been slain, yet they live (Rev 5:6; 13:3)[3]
- Both receive worldwide worship (Rev 5:8–9; 13:4)
- Both have followers who receive a name on their foreheads (Rev 13:16; 14:1)

More parallels could be listed.[4] For now, we can observe why many would identify this beast as "anti-Christ." He is a false messiah who, like the true one, receives worship and seeks to rule the nations (Rev 13:7–8; cf. 12:5). As he ruled, the beast would also pursue the woman and her children for forty-two months.

That time line of three and a half years appears in several forms in Revelation: forty-two months (Rev 11:2; 13:5); 1,250 days (11:3; 12:6); a time, times, and a half a time (12:14). The repetition is significant. It shows

---

3. It is significant that the injuries of both the Lamb and the sea beast are predicated with the same verb in Greek (slain) even though they are translated differently in English. English Bibles often imply the beast's head was merely wounded, whereas the Greek draws a more obvious parallel to the Lamb in that both the beast and Lamb were "slain."

4. See Beale and Campbell, *Revelation: A Shorter Commentary*, 271.

that the trampling of the temple (11:2), the ministry of the two witnesses (11:3), the woman's hiding in the wilderness (12:6), and the beast's authority (13:5) all overlap. These passages depict a spiritual battle between God's people and the beast. This battle is limited, or cut short (three and a half is half the number of perfection) because the church's battle is not an eternal one. Even more importantly, it is not the true battle. It is only a proxy war for a deeper one between the dragon and the Lamb.

In this proxy war, Christians may well end up like Antipas of Pergamum or the two witnesses (Rev 2:13; 11:7). Nevertheless, even as the temple—the church—is trampled, God's people find refuge and spiritual protection while the beast wages his war. These are the ones whose names are written in the Lamb's Book of Life (13:8).

Who or What Is the Sea-Beast?

Interpreters have spent much energy attempting to identify the beast and to decipher the cryptic number of his name in Rev 13:16–18. It is a centuries old tradition to try to hit this curveball, but those who step up to the plate have a zero-batting average. In the United States, readers of Revelation have identified virtually every president in recent history as the antichrist. When possible, they try to tie in the number 666 (e.g., "Ronald Wilson Reagan" has three words with six letters). Part of the difficulty is that creative mathematics, the reader's political agenda, and a superficial knowledge of numerology can find hidden 666s everywhere.

An important starting point for us is the question of how John's readers made sense of his imagery. They certainly would not have been thinking in terms of an American president. The scope of Revelation is more broad than the homeland of the few of its interpreters who happen to reside in the United States of America.

A Christian living in Pergamum would find natural parallels between the beast and her own life. Pergamum was the seat of the imperial cult in the province of Asia. It was the place where "Satan's throne is" (Rev 2:13). If that Pergamene Christian was familiar with the goings on in Rome surrounding the reign of Nero, further connections to the beast would emerge. Rome exercised great, worldwide authority. It demanded worship and it stood behind many of the evils that God's people experienced.

Even so, Rome also experienced political instability following Nero's demise. Between 68–69 CE, four would-be emperors claimed the throne and Vespasian eventually won out. In the midst of all this, rumors abounded that Nero had resurrected, or that he had never truly died. Many commentators believe the slain and healed head in Rev 13:3 alludes to such rumors about Nero. Along these lines, the number 666 seems connected to the words "Nero Caesar." When those Greek words are transcribed into Hebrew characters, the sum of the letters is 666 (each Hebrew letter carries a numerical value).

Was Nero—or Rome—the antichrist? It is a matter of perspective. He certainly was anti-Christ and anti-Christ's followers. Nero was the emperor who used Christians as human torches to illuminate his garden parties. Even so, the beast from the sea in Rev 13 is also larger than Nero and Rome. In other words, just as Egypt sat for the portrait of the dragon (see above), Rome and Nero sat for the portrait of the beast. "John is warning his readers that the evil that was incarnate in Nero is not finished yet."[5]

Has the Beast Come, Or Is He Coming?

This understanding of the beast leaves unanswered the question regarding a future ruler who is the dragon's false messiah. That may very well be. We must also remember that 1 John 2:18 indicated the existence of many antichrists who have arrived with false teaching about Jesus (cf. 2 John 7). Granted, the letters of John and Rev 13 may not be describing the same topic. The point remains, however: the identity of people as dictators, elected representatives, charismatic leaders of a populace, or even members of a local congregation is inconsequential. When they adopt a mentality that demands our loyalty and deflects focus off of Jesus and onto themselves, an antichrist spirit is at work.

In John's time, this evil manifested itself as Rome and its emperors' claims to divinity. In our time, it appears different. In the future, it may take another form. In every case it will appear alluring. This calls for caution on the part of Christians, especially for Christians who concede that our churches do not resemble the "good" (persecuted) churches of Smyrna and Philadelphia. If our context is actually more akin to the situations of the churches in Pergamum, Sardis, and Ephesus, we must also recognize that sin is not just "out there" in the world. Rather, it is close at home and looks appealing and sensible to us. Of course, lurking underneath the surface is the spiritual issue: worship (Rev 13:4, 8; cf. v. 15). Who or what do we

5. Reddish, *Revelation*, 251.

worship? What do we cherish that also demands supremacy in our lives alongside the Lamb? Who or what owns our devotion? How Christians live their lives and follow in Jesus' footsteps reveals more about the answer to these questions than our words or how we spend our Sundays.

Because Christians cannot share worship, the beast waged war against the saints (Rev 11:7; 13:7). This has happened both in John's time and our own. Once something lays claim to our allegiance, the exclusiveness of Scripture's command that God's people worship him—and him alone—cannot be tolerated. That is what leads to the forty-two-month-long struggle with the beast (Rev 13:5).

John's description of the beast concludes with a warning: "If anyone is destined for captivity, to captivity he goes; if anyone kills with the sword, with the sword he must be killed. Here is the perseverance and the faith of the saints" (13:10). In their battle with the beast, the saints persevere not through militant opposition, nor through panic and avoiding trials. Rather, through patient endurance and faithfully witnessing about Jesus, God's people claim a true victory and take part in defeating the dragon. Faith overcomes the beast, but it is the humble faith of the persecuted.

The Beast from the Earth

Whereas the beast from the sea parodied Jesus, the one from the earth is a counterfeit church. The later designation of this beast as a false prophet reveals his religious nature and contrasts with the church's prophetic witness (see Rev 19:20; 20:10). Whereas the church points to the Lamb, the earth beast points people to the false messiah: the sea beast.

If the first beast personalized the evil of empire and government—or any entity—that claims lordship for itself, the second beast reflects the religious establishment that sanctions such entities. When religion gets into bed with the state and grasps for earthly power, faithfulness to the Lamb goes out the window. States are happy to designate authority to religions willing to serve the state.

The requirement to worship the sea beast through its idols reflects the situation early Christians faced when imperial religion demanded their worship (Rev 13:15). Pressure to pay homage to the emperor in Asia Minor was extreme. By the end of the first century, virtually every city had some sort of sanctuary honoring the emperor. Citizens were pressured to display their allegiance to Rome through offering sacrifices on festival days. It was advertised as patriotism, but underneath patriotism's mask lurked idolatry.

In addition to directing people into false worship, the earth beast legitimated its claims with signs, just as the church—the two witnesses—did in chapter 11. Like the witnesses, the earth-beast called down fire from heaven. He performed great signs demonstrating the "truth" of the sea beast's apparent resurrection (13:14). Unlike the church, however, the earth beast advanced worship of the state, not the Lamb. It accomplished this through the use of an idol that it made alive (13:15). That ability may refer either to chicanery (common in ancient Roman religions, especially when people sought oracles) or to demonic activity.

While all of that is intriguing, the measure of a true prophet is not one's ability to perform signs; it is one's commitment to pointing people toward the true God. John's readers recognized this beast as a deceiver by the fruit he produced. He was the propaganda machine that convinces people they have not forsaken God. The earth beast manipulates people into unknowingly surrendering their faith so that they accept the speaker's fabricated narrative as true. In so doing, the false prophet slyly turns worshipers away from the Lamb to the beast.

Perhaps the greatest way the earth beast wields his authority is in exerting pressure on people to identify themselves as devotees of the sea beast. He fashioned a mark required for buying and selling. This mark of the beast has occupied readers' attention since Revelation was first read aloud. More recently, it has been identified as vaccines, social security cards, credit cards, etc. Significantly, none of these really connect to the identity of the beast. These interpretations ignore that Rev 13:16–18 associates the mark with the beast's name (see above).

In light of the larger message of Revelation, it is remarkable that Christians exert extraordinary energy trying to decipher the mark that identifies one as a follower of the beast when in actuality the mark in Revelation that should concern us most is the seal of Christ (Rev 7:1–3). Avoidance of the beast does not make us holy; identification with Christ does—that is our goal. When the church follows Jesus faithfully, we will not accidentally surrender our loyalty to him. What does it say about us as readers when we spend such disproportionate amounts of time contemplating and meditating on the demonic in Revelation rather than heeding its call to worship the Lamb?

As with Jesus' seal that the church received on its forehead (Rev 7:1–8; 14:1), the mark of the beast is likely a nonphysical mark. It symbolizes a person's willingness to compromise loyalty to the Lamb for life with the beast. That was the problem created by imperial worship in John's time. Refusal to worship Rome made day-to-day life harder. It became difficult to procure food and to make a living without adopting some of the empire's idolatry. The church then, as today, had to remain vigilant to ensure its loyalty was indivisible.

Religion and Politics

The work of the dragon and his two accomplices is terrifying: evil puts on flesh and leads people away from God. Even more concerning is the point that this trifecta of evil is limited neither to Rome in the first century, nor to some future "Rome." Apocalyptic literature addresses the readers's present. The evil we encounter in Rev 13 manifests itself in our own time just as it did in John's time. A temptation always exists to identify the sea beast with someone else. Totalitarian governments (Nazi Germany, Iran, China, and North Korea) make easy targets for seeing the beast at work. Especially in places where state-sanctioned Christianity follows governmental guidelines regarding how the gospel is presented, it does not take much imagination to see the two beasts working together to glorify the dragon.

All of that being said, while such interpretations may be correct, neither do they constitute the whole truth. The beasts also lurk in the democratic western hemisphere. Politicians pressure Christians to surrender the full teaching of Scripture for a political platform. They promise cultural influence through compromise in doctrine and do deliver, but their power is not Lamb power; it is the beastly power. The beast's influence is seen in the propaganda that demonizes and denigrates those who do not agree with "us," which stands in stark contrasts to Jesus' sacrificial death on behalf of those who opposed him.

Propaganda manipulates Christians into believing political disagreement is theological disagreement and that political opponents are therefore enemies of the faith. Among the tirades and rhetoric that pervade mainstream and social media, one must remember the proverb "when words are many, transgression is not lacking" (Prov 10:19). The beasts work tirelessly to germinate disagreements among Christians and to produce divisions and factions. They cultivate within us an inordinate love of things and people besides Jesus. Ultimately, the success of the beasts is seen in a compromised witness about Jesus. A church known by its politics as opposed to the transformation that the Holy Spirit does in its midst cannot witness in the same way Christians in Smyrna and Philadelphia did. We will not find Antipas of Pergamum in a church that has abandoned the gospel; he will move elsewhere.

When Christians succeed in refusing to split their allegiance, they incur harsh opposition. The dragon and the two beasts will continue their war against God's people. The beast of the sea will wield the power of the state. The beast of the earth will perform signs to convince us of truth in what is false. As such things occur, all signs point toward defeat of the church. Christians die and the empire wins. On this side of heaven, when Christians look at our situation, we can respond with despair. Everything looks wrong and those who know what is right are ostracized or persecuted. That is the picture painted by Rev 13.

5. But Wait, There's More! (Revelation 14:1–20)

Out of the gloom and desperation of Rev 13, hope arises from the opening words of chapter 14. John saw the entire world forced into idolatry and worship of the beast, but then his gaze shifted: "I looked, and behold! The Lamb..." (Rev 14:1, author's translation). What follows in Rev 14 contrasts the despair experienced on earth with a heavenly perspective that reveals Jesus and the church (vv. 1–5), proclaims an angelic sermon (vv. 6–13), and narrates God's judgment (vv. 14–20).

The Lamb and His People (Revelation 14:1–5)

John saw Jesus standing on Mount Zion (Jerusalem). As the city in which God had chosen to dwell, Jews believed Jerusalem was the focal point of God's eschatological salvation. Through its temple—God's dwelling place—Jerusalem was the special connecting point between heaven and earth. It also became a focal point for Christianity since Jerusalem was where Jesus died and resurrected, inaugurating God's ultimate salvation of his people. The Lamb standing on Mount Zion also anticipates the heavenly New Jerusalem that John will see in Rev 21–22, where God's people live in communion with him.

Revelation 14:1–5 offers the alternate apocalyptic perspective to what John saw in Rev 12–13. Jesus stands in the place of God's salvation and with him we also find his people: the 144,000. They have persevered despite their apparent defeat in the war with the beast. As we saw before, the 144,000 represent all of God's people (see discussion of Rev 7:1–17 in chapter 6).

The presence of Jesus' and his Father's name on the 144,000 supports the notion that they are Jesus' followers (cf. Rev 22:3–4). The mark of the name corresponds to the seal of protection the church received in Rev 7:2–8 and it is the heavenly counterpoint to the mark of the beast, which was likewise associated with the beast's name (13:17; 14:9, 11). In both cases, the mark identifies one's lord: one can belong to the Messiah, or to the anti-Messiah.

Revelation 14:1–5 demonstrates that—despite all appearances—those marked as belonging to Jesus become victorious and are engaged in worship. Having heard the arrogant words and blasphemies of the sea beast and his worshipers in Rev 13, we now experience the truth proclaimed in the old hymn: "Hark! How the heavenly anthem drowns all music but its own!"[6] Such is the praise of the church that is purchased from the earth (Rev 5:9–10; 14:3). It resounds in heaven before the throne and throughout heavenly court.

Revelation 14:4–5 also adds the perplexing description of God's people as undefiled and virgins. If the 144,000 number is symbolic, then it is likely that the description of that same group in vv. 4–5 is likewise symbolic. It is a safe assumption that John does not believe God's people should remain chaste.

Context is needed when interpreting the language of defilement. The Old Testament regularly portrayed Israel as a virgin who defiled herself through idolatry. Inappropriate worship described metaphorically as illicit sexual activity appears in Revelation too. Revelation 14:8 identifies Babylon as a source of (sexual) immorality (cf. 17:2–4; 18:1–3). Additionally, Jesus connected the false teachings of Balaam and Jezebel with the same immorality (Rev 2:14, 20–22). In each of these passages, the problem was idolatry, not sex. In contrast to the world's theological adultery, God's people kept themselves as pure virgins awaiting their wedding with the Lamb (Rev 14:4; 19:9; 21:2, 9).

Another layer of meaning to the sexual imagery arises from Israel's military practice. In the Old Testament, Israelite armies at times refrained

---

6. Bridges, "Crown Him with Many Crowns."

from sexual activity (e.g., 1 Sam 21:4–5) since sexual intercourse generated minor amounts ritual impurity (Lev 15:16–18). This is not to say the Old Testament construed sex as sinful (impurity and sin are distinct in Leviticus). Rather, it rendered one unfit for participation in religious services. Armies would refrain from sexual activity because wars were religious affairs.

Revelation 14 appropriates this imagery to communicate that God's people constitute a heavenly army that follows the Lamb wherever he goes (14:4; 19:14). This army has an odd battle plan, however. It's general died willingly and sacrificially and so must his followers. The most notable place the Lamb went was the cross and the church follows him. As followers of the Lamb, they remain blameless and are identified along with Jesus in fulfilling the prophecy that no lie was found in the Messiah's mouth (Rev 14:5; cf. Zeph 3:13; Isa 53:9).

An Angelic Sermon (Revelation 14:6–13)

John listened as angels proclaimed the story that has echoed through the centuries. Put plainly, Rev 14:6–13 shares a three-part sermon told by angels about the hope of salvation and humanity's need for repentance as the world careens toward judgment.

This is a good news sermon because people may yet escape God's wrath if they repent and worship God. That is the message proclaimed by the first angel (Rev 14:6–7). Everyone on earth, from each tribe, language, and ethnic group heard the prophetic call to fear and glorify God. This worldwide group was also the same populace that looked upon the corpses of the two witnesses and that followed the beast (11:9; 13:7). They now receive a final call to worship the one true God who made everything because the hour of judgment has arrived.

In light of the first angel's call to fear God, the second angel proclaimed that the place from which people seek security—Babylon, John's label for Rome—was already defeated (Rev 14:8). Like Israel's prophets, John spoke about what God was about to accomplish in the past tense: Babylon has fallen (past tense), but she hasn't realized it yet. She is still busy getting people drunk on the wine of idolatry (14:8; cf. 17:2). Jeremiah also attributed this intoxicating behavior to Babylon in the sixth century BCE (Jer 51:7). Empires tempt people to worship the state by giving it their allegiance in exchange for security. Doing so does occasionally bring temporary security and even economic prosperity under the rule of the beasts, but drinking from that cup also intoxicates the worshiper, leaving her unable to worship the true God.

Consequently, those who imbibe Babylon's idolatrous wine will also drink from the cup of God's wrath. That is the message of the third angel (Rev 14:9–12). The wine of God's punishment for sin has been mixed to full strength and those who have chosen to reject the Lamb and to identify with the beast will be tormented with fire and brimstone. Various perspectives within the Christian faith debate what is symbolic or literal in this imagery and whether God's eternal punishment is an ultimate removal and obliteration of sinners, or an eternal conscious existence under God's wrath.

The similarities between the fate of those who worshiped the beast (Rev 14:9–11) and the fate of the beasts and dragon themselves (Rev 20:10) pushes against the conclusion that God's punishment amounts to reducing sinners to nonexistence. It is neither a pleasant nor popular message that the angel of Rev 14 proclaims, but the torment mentioned in v. 11 never appears in Scripture as meaning anything besides suffering. This is why the angels of Rev 14:6–13 offer people a last chance to repent.

The escape from this horrible end appears in Rev 14:12–13. Salvation comes to the saints who endure by keeping God's commands and who follow Jesus faithfully. These too will suffer and even die, but that is also the path to victory and to resting from the labors of faithfully following Jesus and proclaiming the gospel (Rev 14:13).

An Initial Look at Judgment (Revelation 14:14–20)

The final verses of Rev 14 provide an initial glimpse of the final judgment. John saw one like a son of man sitting on a cloud with a sickle. This is probably a picture of Christ drawing from Dan 7:13. In the Old Testament, God's presence commonly manifested itself as a cloud (Exod 40:34–38; Num 9:15–22; 12:5; Deut 31:15). Writings toward the end of the Old Testament period also connect the day of God's judgment with a combination of God's presence and cloudiness (Lam 2:1; Nah 1:3; Zeph 1:14–15).

In Rev 14:14–15, Jesus arrived in judgment and an angel announced that the time arrived for reaping—judging—the earth. Once the son of man sent his sickle over the earth, a second harvest happened when another angel with a sharp sickle reaped the grapes of the earth so they could be trod in the winepress of God's wrath (Rev 14:17–20).

Readers of Revelation disagree regarding whether this passage envisions two distinct harvests or one two-part harvest. The possibility of two harvests encourages some to see an allusion to a rapture of the faithful in the first harvest whereas the second harvest is the judgment of sinners.

That is one way of reading the text, but it is not the only one and several factors point against a harvest of the faithful in Rev 14:14–16. The command given to the son of man says the "hour" has come (v. 15). Significantly, almost every other time the Greek word "hour" appears in Revelation, it is in the context of judgment in the sense of punishment (see, Rev 3:3; 9:15; 11:13; 14:7; 18:10, 17, 19). Additionally, there is an Old Testament text that connects the ideas of harvesting, treading grapes in a winepress, and God's judgment. In Joel 3:13, these concepts coalesce in a prophecy about the enemies of God's people. Similarly, when Jesus' parable of the wheat and weeds spoke about gathering at harvest time, the primary object of the gathering was the weeds destined for the fire (Matt 13:24–30, 36–43).

Given that judgment has been a major theme within the context of Rev 14, the above factors suggest that the harvest in vv. 14–16 is a gathering of the wicked. Along these same lines, the reaping of the grapes in vv. 17–20 may retell the same story of judgment in a different manner. Or, if these verses do narrate a separate harvest, it is one that symbolizes a preparation for judgment. Since God's judgment is symbolized as wine, John says that all the grapes were reaped to communicate the full extent of God's wrath. Some think this is also the point of saying that the "blood," or juice, ran 1,600 stadia (over 180 miles) outside the city. The figure of 1,600 is produced when multiplying the squares of four and ten, both of which were numeric symbols of completion.

6. Conclusion

Revelation 12–14 has covered an extensive terrain. Chapter 12 summarized the entirety of the Church Age as God's people await deliverance in the wilderness while the beast rages. Chapter 13 introduced the beasts of the sea and earth who functioned as proxies that perform the will of the dragon. Together, the three form a sort of unholy trinity that manifest the powers of Satan, empire, and idolatry in a sustained campaign to alienate and exterminate the people of God.

Nevertheless, hope arises. As the situation became desperate beyond hope in Rev 12–13, John turned his gaze heavenward and saw the Lamb standing on Mt. Zion in 14:1. What followed was a picture of the church triumphant and a proclamation of a final message to the world to repent before the final arrival of God's judgment.

Although many Christians seldom read more than one chapter of Revelation at a time, Rev 12–14 is one passage of Scripture. Each section fits together to form a coherent message in which John once again gives two perspectives of a complex reality. From the perspective of earth, it will appear that the dragon wins. The empire of the sea beast possesses power and all the nations drink that power and align with it in ways that God's people cannot condone. The church appears defeated. But that is not the entire picture. John offers an alternative apocalyptic perspective that reminds the faithful that the Lamb is coming and God's judgment will set the world right as injustice is removed.

To the faithful, Rev 12–14 gives hope. The temptation will always be for readers to identify themselves with the church in these chapters. But we must also hear the troubling words of Rev 12–14 as addressed to us. The church must remain wary of false teachings and take caution to avoid aligning itself with the beasts. The prophetic call to fear God and give him glory is addressed to all who dwell on the earth, not only the unchurched. It is a reminder to Christians in Ephesus, Thyatira, and Sardis to wake up before it is too late.

Let those who have ears hear what the Spirit says to the churches.

For Further Study

Discussion Questions

1. If Rev 12 symbolized the life of the church as a life of hiding in the wilderness, in what ways does that correspond to your life? How might your journey, individually or with your faith community, feel like a trek through the wilderness?

2. The beasts of Rev 13 correspond closely to the power of the state (empire) and false religion. Often these two powers work in tandem, tempting Christians to combine their faith with external forces (e.g., admiration of people and platforms alongside Jesus). Where do you see Christians tempted to combine our faith with non-Christian entities? Where are you tempted to do this?

3. Revelation 14 offers hope as Jesus appears in victory, but that scene quickly gives way to the treading of the grapes for God's judgment. In what ways can we see God's love and mercy in Rev 14 and what might it teach us about those concepts?

10

Outpouring God's Justice

Preparatory reading:

- Revelation 15–16

1. Introduction

Have you ever watched a movie with so many sub-plots that it took forever to conclude? Sometimes a story is so complex and there are so many lines running concurrently in the plot that it feels like a movie ends three or four times before the credits finally roll.

Revelation sometimes feels like one of those movies. The seventh trumpet introduced the last judgment and announced that God's kingdom had arrived (Rev 11:15–19). But then there was more to the story. John saw a great sign in Rev 12:1 as he witnessed the woman's struggle with the dragon. That story seemed to conclude as Rev 14 proclaimed Babylon's fall and narrated the final judgment (Rev 14:17–20), but the credits haven't yet begun to roll. In Rev 15–16, readers receive another angle for understanding God's judgment of sin and its effects on creation.

As we observed with the trumpet judgments, Revelation does not narrate a linear chronology. Reading Revelation is like using the lenses of a microscope that zoom progressively deeper and deeper to reveal how deep the problem of sin runs. Or, we might compare the different judgments of Revelation to a pianist's ability to strike several tones simultaneously.

As John weaves the various strands of Revelation together, we again find substantial overlap between the bowl judgments of chapter 16, the trumpet judgments, and the story of Exodus. Once again, Revelation will depict the deliverance of God's people and the judgment of sin.

2. The Song of Deliverance (Revelation 15:1–4)

The initial verses of Revelation 15 occupy an important transition point within the book. In one sense, they conclude a series of seven visions that began in chapter 12. As such, Revelation 15:1–4 wraps up the story of God's people in their struggle with the dragon and his beasts.

Simultaneously, Rev 15:1–4 opens a new section of Revelation by introducing the seven final plagues. By mentioning those plagues alongside the Song of Moses in v. 3, Revelation looks in two directions. It anticipates the catastrophes that await in the bowl judgments of Rev 16 while also remembering the trumpet judgments (sometimes called plagues; cf. Rev 9:18, 20) and the plagues of Exodus.

Worship was crucial in the Exodus story. God's stated purpose for bringing Israel out of Egypt was so that they could worship him. That is what became possible when he led them through the Red Sea in Exod 14. Just as God's people stood victorious on the far side of the Red Sea, John saw a victorious people standing on a glassy sea mixed with fire (Rev 15:2; cf. Exod 15:1–20). The mixture of the sea with fire implies it is related to God's judgment (cf. Rev 8:5, 7–8; 9:17–18; 11:5; 14:10; 19:20; 20:9–10, 14). Nevertheless, the posture of the people is one of victory: they stand over this sea mixed with fire.

Ancient cosmology understood that above the earth and the expanse of the sky was water that separated the realm of the divine from the earth. In Rev 15:2, God's people have passed through that sea in a new—spiritual—exodus. The connection to the Exodus story is confirmed by the reference to the Song of Moses in v. 3.

After Israel passed through the Red Sea, they sang and praised God for his deliverance (Exod 15:1–18). That passage continues to occupy a special place in Jewish liturgy. It is the ultimate song of God's deliverance, which is why Torah scrolls have special regulations for formatting the song. The Hebrew song is written in thirty lines that resemble half bricks stacked on top of full bricks.[1] Revelation apparently alluded to this song when it

---

1. Rabinowitz, "Sea, Song of the."

mentioned the Song of Moses. The song reminds us that the God worshiped in Revelation is the God of deliverance in Exodus.

Interestingly, while Revelation points to Exod 15, the words reported in Rev 15:3–4 do not come from any single passage in the Old Testament. Of its forty-eight Greek words, thirty-eight come from several parts of the Old Testament:

- The song opens with a description of God's great and marvelous works, recalling Greek versions of Deut 11:7; 28:59 and Ps 111:1–4 (LXX Ps 110:2–4).
- God's righteousness and holiness echo the Greek version of Deut 32:4, which is also called a Song of Moses.
- Extolling God as the King of the nations and asking who does not fear him parallels Jer 10:7.
- In Ps 86:9, all the nations worship and glorify God's name.
- The theme of all nations coming to God also appears in Psalm 86:9 and is a prominent theme in the prophets (cf. Isa 2:3; Mic 4:2; Zech 8:20–23; 14:16)

The song of Rev 15:3–4 is a symphony of the Old Testament witness. It combines various poetic and prophetic Scriptures to glorify God's great miracles, sovereignty, God's characteristics of justice and truth, his holiness, and the fact that the nations will ultimately recognize this and worship God. That is the effect of God's judgments and is why God's victorious people joyfully proclaimed the revelation of God's righteous judgments (Rev 15:4).[2] God's action set aright everything that had gone wrong.

As with many other places in Revelation, the starting point for understanding chapters 15–16 is worship. God is worthy of worship because of who he is and because of how God has revealed his justice to correct a broken world. Even so, the trumpet judgments have already demonstrated that the prospect of moving from dysfunctionality to spiritual wholeness can be incredibly painful. It is painful to choose to worship the one who is worthy when people have spent their lives with allegiances elsewhere. That

---

2. Here, the KJV's "judgments" is preferable to many modern translations. The Greek word does describe God's righteous actions (NASB, ESV), but the semantic range of the word first and foremost relates to judgment (cf. NRSV, CEB; see also Liddell et al., "Δικαίωμα," 429).

is why many will refuse to fear and recognize God and why Rev 16 reports a very terrifying sequence of judgments.

3. Introducing Another Round of Judgment (Revelation 15:5-8)

Following the worship of vv. 3-4, John's vision evokes Israel's time in the wilderness: "The sanctuary of the tent of the witness in heaven was opened" (Rev 15:5, author's translation). The phrase "tent of witness" never appears in the Old Testament, but it recalls the tent of meeting Israel used in the wilderness (Exod 33:7-11; 40:35). In that tent, Moses met God and received direction. Revelation 15 now reveals a heavenly version of that meeting place.

Emerging from the place of God's dwelling in the heavenly temple came seven angels with the seven final plagues. Each received a bowl filled with God's wrath from one of the living creatures from Rev 4.

The picture of the angels and their bowls combines two prominent Old Testament themes. First, the angels's origination in the sanctuary and their linen attire suggest they served a priestly role, acting on behalf of God. Accordingly, the bowls resembled religious implements used in Israelite worship (Exod 27:3; 38:3; 1 Kgs 7:45; 2 Chr 4:8; Zech 9:15; cf. Rev 5:8). The word for "bowl" in Rev 15 and denotes a small saucer that could be used for pouring out drink offerings, or for imbibing wine or some other drink.

In Zech 9:15, God's people drank in celebration of God's deliverance. Along with that deliverance, God's judgment upon the nations was prominent in that passage. This introduces the second Old Testament theme in Rev 15:5-8: judgment. In addition to any liturgical function the bowls have, they also bring another round of judgment, just as the cup of God's wrath did in the Old Testament (Isa 51:17; Jer 49:12; cf. Ref 14:10).

Revelation 15 concluded with smoke filling the temple so that nobody could enter until the priestly angels completed their work of pouring out the last judgments. Smoke symbolized God's presence, resembling the pillar of cloud that filled the tent in the wilderness and prevented Moses from entering to meet with God (Exod 40:35). In Revelation, the filling of the temple with smoke communicates that these final judgments originate with God. It may also very well be that the prevention of anyone from entering the sanctuary suggests the judgments will not be interrupted or cut short.

4. Pouring the Bowls (Revelation 16:1–21)

Like the trumpet judgments, the bowls proceed at a rapid pace once a loud voice commanded them to be poured out (Rev 16:1). Additionally by following a similar progression to the trumpets, the bowls also exhibit parallels to the plagues of Exodus. Significantly, both the bowl and trumpet judgments are called plagues in Revelation. The overlap between the bowls and trumpets is one reason some interpreters believe the different series of judgments in Revelation occur simultaneously rather than sequentially. The bowls retell the story of the trumpets from a different angle.

Bowls 1–3 (Revelation 16:2–7)

The localities under judgment in the first three bowls repeat the progression of the initial three trumpets (Rev 8:7–11). In each sequence, the initial judgment was directed at the earth. Unlike the first trumpet, though, the first bowl did not destroy vegetation but rather inflicted painful sores on those who have committed idolatry.

The second bowl and trumpet each targeted the sea. Whereas the trumpet destroyed a third of the life in the sea, the bowl annihilated all life (perhaps including sailors) and turned the sea into blood. This judgment probably anticipates the condemnation of Rome's economics in Rev 18 and may symbolize its collapse. Maritime trade served the empire well and the removal of such trade becomes a source of lament for the mariners in Rev 18:17–19.

The third bowl, like the third trumpet, struck and contaminated the earth's fresh water systems. Once John saw earth's fresh water turn bloody, he heard two things: a hymn of praise sung by the "angel of the waters" and a voice from the altar that likewise praised God. The song of the angel declared that God is righteous and named him as "the one who is and who was, the Holy One" (16:5, author's translation).

That nomenclature is important. Revelation began with God worshiped as "the one who is, and who was, and who is to come" (Rev 1:4, 8; 4:8). As of Rev 11:17, he is no longer the one who is coming; God has arrived. Revelation 16:5 emphasizes this point by replacing "who is to come" with "the Holy One." The temple has opened, God's presence has emerged in judgment, and the waters proclaimed his justice in these judgments.

The voice emanating from the altar in Rev 16:7 is that of the martyrs (Rev 6:9–11). They previously cried out asking God how long before he would avenge their blood. Now, they say, "Yes, Lord God Almighty, true and righteous are your judgments" (16:7, author's translation).

The praise of the angel of the waters and of the martyrs declare that God's punishments in the initial bowl judgments fit the crime. This is a principle one finds in non-biblical apocalypses too. For instance, a book known as the Apocalypse of Peter, which many Christians read between the second and fourth centuries, imagined several punishments sinners encounter in hell that correspond to their transgressions in life:

- Blasphemers were hung up by their tongues over fire, or gnawed their own lips.

- Men who committed adultery were "hung up by their feet" (perhaps a euphemism for "hung by their genitals").

- Wealthy men and women who ignored orphans and widows were left to roll around in filthy garments.[3]

Likewise, in Rev 16:2–7 idolaters who received the mark of the beast and worshiped his image receive a new mark: the painful sores of the first bowl. Similarly, when the earth's water congealed into blood, the angel declared that God's judgment fit the crime: those who poured out the blood of God's saints and prophets received blood to drink.

Bowls 4–5 (Revelation 16:8–11)

Shifting away from earth's landscape, the fourth and fifth bowls impact its heat and light. The fourth bowl inflicted the opposite effect of the fourth trumpet. Whereas the trumpet darkened the sun (Rev 8:12), the bowl ramped up its power, thereby scorching people who in turn refused to repent. Conversely, the fifth bowl plunged the beast's throne and kingdom into darkness.

Commentators debate whether the bowl judgments are literal or symbolic. Either way, their point is difficult to miss: normal life screeches to a halt as God brings an end to evil. We can see this especially with the fourth bowl. If the sun's scorching heat is literal, it would appear the worst fears of those sounding an alarm about climate change become realized. This would

---

3. "Apocalypse of Peter," 145–46.

have massive implications that ripple across all sectors of life. Parts of the planet would become uninhabitable and economies would collapse. If the heat is figurative, it recalls symbolic language from the Old Testament that illustrated God's judgment in terms of fire (cf. Deut 32:22; Ps 18:7–8; Lam 4:11). Either way, the point remains that those who come under judgment reap the exact opposite of what was promised to the faithful in Rev 7:16.

The fifth bowl did not primarily target the sun, but attacked the throne of the beast, which may symbolize a disruption of his ability to rule. The result of that judgment was a universal version of the fourth trumpet (and ninth Egyptian plague): darkness. In Rev 8:12, one third of the day became dark; in the fourth bowl, that palpable darkness becomes all-encompassing.

With both the fourth and fifth bowls, people remained obstinate in their refusal to repent. Rather than glorifying God (as with the seventh trumpet, Rev 11:13), they blasphemed—they spoke against the God who had authority over the plagues (Rev 16:9, 11). The judgments apparently overlapped one another since the people remained afflicted by the sores of the first bowl even as the fifth had been poured out. The cumulative effect of the first five bowls was that people refused to acknowledge God, just as Pharaoh refused in Exodus.

Mitchell Reddish points out that the judgments of Revelation can serve both retributive and penitential roles.[4] In other words, they can bring punishment and retribution for one's sin, or they can occasion penitence and thereby turn people back to God. In the case of the bowls (and the first six trumpets), people reaped the punishment for sin almost exclusively. There was no desire to repent.

God allows ample time and opportunity to recognize evil for what it is. He provides time for repentance and sends the church as his witnesses. There is opportunity to repent and follow the Lamb, but the bowls show that people refuse that opportunity and elect to continue in speaking against God.

Bowls 6–7 (Revelation 16:12–21)

The final two bowls describe the events preceding the return of Christ and in this also recapitulate the events of the sixth and seventh trumpets. Significantly, though, Revelation is also intentional to communicate that while these verses speak to a future that was removed from the first century, the

---

4. Reddish, *Revelation*, 306.

contents of these verses nonetheless remain meaningful and instructive for the church through the ages by calling followers of Christ to faithfulness.

The Sixth Bowl

A number of parallels connect the sixth bowl with the sixth trumpet:

Table 3 Parallels Between the Sixth Bowl and Sixth Trumpet		
	Trumpet 6 (Rev 9:13–21)	Bowl 6 (Rev 16:12–16)
The number three	Plagues of fire, smoke, and brimstone	Dragon, beast, and false prophet
Location	The Euphrates River	The Euphrates River
Importance of mouths	Horsemen kill with plagues emanating from their mouths and their mouths "do harm"	Spirits emerge from the mouth of the dragon, beast, and false prophet
Demonic Action:	The demons kill one-third of humanity	The demons perform signs

The similarities between the two events imply that each one constitutes a variation on the theme of eschatological disaster that accompanies the final judgment. Whereas the sixth trumpet summons a deadly army from the east that kills people, the bowl is the harbinger of demons that unite people against the Lamb and gather them at *Har-Magedon*. Those demons emanate from the mouths of the trio of evil we encountered in Rev 12–13: the dragon, the sea beast, and the earth beast. The last of these is now identified more precisely as a false prophet, which fits his role in Rev 13:13–14.

The description of the spirits as frogs may reflect the ritually unclean status Leviticus ascribed to the amphibians, but Revelation more likely draws its imagery from the plague of frogs in Exodus. This time, however, it is not a swarm of literal frogs, but three spirits that perform signs and gather people for war against God. Their ability to deceive with signs might remind readers of Jesus' warning that false prophets would come with miracles in the last days (Matt 24:24).

The drying up of the Euphrates River resembles some of God's greatest acts of salvation in the Old Testament: the splitting of the Red Sea (Exod 14) and the stopping of the Jordan River (Josh 3). In this case, though, the drying of the Euphrates serves the purpose of judgment, not salvation. This is not some new Exodus-type event; it was a threat readily recognized by John's Roman readers. The Euphrates constituted the border of the Roman empire with Parthia. Consequently, its drying up created a pathway for the kings of the east to invade (see discussion of the sixth trumpet in chapter 7).

John does not dwell on the identity of the kings of the east (Rev 16:12), or of the kings of the world (v. 14). The two groups seem distinct, but readers can lose the larger picture of John's message by dwelling on the details of different identities. The gathering of the nations deploys a prominent Old Testament theme wherein God would gather the enemies of his people for judgment and subsequently would establish himself as King (Joel 3:2; Zeph 3:8; Zech 14:1–9).

The location of the gathering has garnered much attention over the years. The best Greek manuscripts of Revelation identify the place as *Har-Magedon*. Bruce Metzger observed that a late Byzantine manuscript was responsible for the popular English spelling *Armageddon*.[5] *Har-Magedon* likely derives from the Hebrew phrase, *har megiddon*, or "Mount Megiddo." Megiddo lied in northern Israel, in a valley inland from Mount Carmel. This valley was the site of many battles (e.g., Judg 4). The city of Megiddo guarded a pass into the central mountains of Canaan and therefore had strategic value.

Although *Har-Magedon* seemingly refers to this place, there is an major deficiency in this reading: there is no Mount Megiddo; the city lies in a valley. Scholars propose several alternate ways to understand the meaning of *Har-Magedon*, but the fascination with finding the place on a map says more about modern readers than John's intention. *What* happens at *Har-Magedon* is more important than *where* it happens. In any case, the *what* question is the focus of John's attention when he says the nations gathered to make war. We will find later that the war ends before it can begin when Jesus returns (Rev 19:11–21).

Together, Rev 16:12–14 and 19:17–21 envision a time when those who reject God will unite as enemies against his people, the church. When this may happen on a global scale is impossible to say. Regardless, it has been the lived experience of many Christians through the centuries. Even before Revelation was written, Christians in Pergamum endured martyrdom. The purpose of Revelation is to encourage such Christians, who should neither be surprised by opposition nor should we attempt to combat it. The revelation of evil is part of God's plan to root out evil. Christians do not fight it in

---

5. Metzger, *Textual Commentary*, 681.

any of the ways that look like fighting, but by remaining faithful followers of the Lamb who was slain.

Revelation 16:15 reorients our focus back onto Jesus and is therefore an important verse to contemplate. It interrupts the flow of John's vision by interjecting a beatitude that blesses those who stay awake and preserve their garments. It warns readers who easily find ourselves lulled to sleep by the world through complacency and the adoption of comfortable lifestyles that go along with the flow of society. Such Christians are the ones Jesus found in Laodicea and Sardis. To Christians being lulled to sleep, Jesus issued a plea to awake because he was coming as a thief (Rev 3:3). Jesus had commanded Laodicean church to buy white garments so that their spiritual nakedness would no longer show itself (3:18). By alluding to both passages in Rev 16:15, Jesus warned the church that the events described here pertain not only to a distant future, but are cause for vigilance even at the time Revelation was written.

The Seventh Bowl

As the sixth bowl and trumpet echoed one another, so do the seventh bowl and trumpet—both narrate history reaching its end.

The seventh bowl employs images we have already seen: lightning, thunder, an earthquake, and hail accompany God's arrival in judgment. Each of these phenomena also appeared with the seventh trumpet, when John heard a voice declaring the advent of God's kingdom (11:15–19; cf. 4:5; 8:5). As the seventh trumpet heralded God's kingdom, the outpouring of the seventh bowl is accompanied by the declaration, "It is finished" bellowing out of the temple and reverberating through heaven. God's judgment had now arrived in its fullness and evil was finally checked.

The apparent epicenter of the earthquake in Rev 16:18–19 was the "great city," Babylon. The ancient city of Babylon was John's label for Rome, which will be called the "great city" several times in the following chapters (Rev 17:18; 18:10, 16, 18–19). The earthquake's division of Rome into three parts symbolized its total destruction. The number three may also foreshadow Rev 18, where John will hear three classes of people lamenting Rome's destruction (kings, merchants, and sailors; 18:9–19). The devastation of the earthquake reminds readers of Rev 6:12–14 in which the sixth seal occasioned an earthquake that removed the hills and islands. God's final judgment has worldwide ramifications.

While Rome was the primary target of John's imagery, one should remember that the scope of Revelation is larger than the first century. Thus, just as Caesar seemingly sat for the portrait of the beast of the sea in Rev 13, Rome becomes a symbolic incarnation of the much larger reality of any empire standing in opposition to God's purposes. More than a city or even a specific nation, one can understand Rome as a way of life in opposition to God and that is what is destroyed by the final judgment.

Despite all that has happened, there is no suggestion about people returning to God in Rev 16. Perhaps due to the deception of the demons of the sixth bowl, they refused to acknowledge God and continued to blaspheme as the beasts of chapter 13 had taught them to do. Rather than repent, they were angered by the hail and continued to speak against God and gathered to make war. In so doing, humanity unwittingly awaits the final judgment, but first John will speak in Rev 17–18 about the destruction of the enemy.

5. Conclusion

The theme of God's justice pervades Rev 15–16 as it reports the final series of eschatological judgments. The scene opened with the victorious faithful singing the Song of Moses that drew on a variety of Old Testament depictions of God and concluded with the statement that his judgments (or, righteous acts) are revealed (15:4). Following this, the angels poured out their bowls and the angel of the waters echoed what the saints had already confessed: God is just and holy and his judgments are true and just (Rev 16:5–7). Despite all of this, humanity remained stalwart in its refusal to concede and confess sin (16:9, 11). It preferred instead to continue to blaspheme God for his punishment of sin (16:21).

Revelation 15–16 warns readers that God's patient waiting for humanity to return to him will eventually end. God will root out sin and establish his kingdom. There will come a time when the voice in the temple will announce, "It is finished." As we wait for that proclamation, the church hears the warning Jesus gave near the end of the sixth bowl: "Behold, I am coming as a thief! Blessed is the one who stays alert and keeps his garments" (16:15, author's translation). The church must remain vigilant in following Christ so that it is not lulled to sleep and one day found naked before God when his judgment comes. Instead, she purchases from Jesus white garments and awaits the bridegroom's return.

For Further Study

Discussion Questions

1. The English words "righteous" and "just" both translate the Greek word *dikaios* in the Song of Moses (Rev 15:3–4). If you read this in your Bible and substitute the word "just" for "righteous" in this song, how does it change its meaning for you?
2. The angels who pour the seven bowls wear priestly attire and serve in the heavenly temple (Rev 15:5–8). How might the bowls of Rev 16 relate to that priestly ministry?
3. In what ways might people observe the events of the fifth and sixth bowls operating in our time?

For Further Reading

- Wright, N. T. *Revelation for Everyone*. Louisville: Westminster John Knox, 2011, 135–48.
- Reddish, Mitchell. *Revelation*. Macon, GA: Smyth & Helwys, 2001, 289–320.

11

Babylon's Demise

Preparatory reading:

- Revelation 17–19
- Ezekiel 26:1—28:19

1. Introduction

When I was in high school, the city of Seattle imploded the Kingdome, which had been the home of the Seattle Seahawks and Mariners for decades. It was the first building implosion I ever watched on TV and the series of sparks and flashes, followed by the building falling in upon itself, captivated me. In mere seconds, what appeared strong and immoveable—indeed, permanent—collapsed into rubble.

That is one way to conceptualize the truth conveyed about Rome (and empires in general) in Rev 17–19. For John's readers, Rome was the immoveable object. It was a fact of life and attempts to remove it were exercises in futility. For many, that was just as well since Rome was also an object of beauty and adoration. It additionally made many people wealthy and powerful.

Personifying all of this beauty, wealth, and power was the goddess Roma who was worshiped far and wide. She commanded the same respect—religious respect—that modern symbols can acquire. The language used about her and the state she represented no doubt resembled language used in modern societies when national icons become threatened. For instance, after rioters briefly occupied the United States Capitol in 2021, House Speaker Nancy Pelosi spoke against the "desecration of this, our temple of democracy—American democracy."[1] Such rhetoric reveals how closely nationalistic zeal can approximate religious sentiment, even with the enduring legacy of the Enlightenment's reluctance to worship all those "silly" gods of the ancient world.

Romans also possessed a religious devotion to their empire and venerated the goddess Roma (and the emperor—who became identified as Zeus/Jupiter). In Rev 17–19, John unveils the true picture of Roma: she was not a beautiful goddess, but a prostitute sitting astride a great beast. Her fate becomes a warning to those tempted to ally themselves with anyone other than the Lamb.

2. An Amazing Sight (Revelation 17:1–6)

One of the angels from Revelation 16 invited John to witness God's judgment of Babylon, already introduced in the bowl judgments. In the wilderness, John saw a woman finely dressed and seated on a beast. The beast resembled the sea beast in Rev 13, possessing seven heads and ten horns (see Rev 13:1).

Revelation identified the woman as a prostitute, but she did not look the part. Her opulent attire bespoke an aristocratic status, if not a royal one. Perhaps, John even intended Roman readers to see a picture of the goddess Roma herself. Evil seldom reveals itself as the grotesque monster; it appears instead as someone very alluring. Even John was greatly amazed when he saw the woman, which was the exact response of those who beheld the sea beast (Rev 13:3).

Evil enthralls. Only on closer inspection do we see the woman's blasphemies and observe that her cup contains abominations and impurities from her prostitution (17:4). She is the "mother of prostitutes and of the abominations of the earth" (Rev 17:5, author's translation). In Greek translations of the Old Testament, the word "abomination" referred not simply to something that was ritually unclean, but was detestable to the point of utter disgust (Lev 20:13; Deut 17:1; 1 Kgs 11:5; 2 Chr 28:3). The word carries that same nuance in Rev 17:5. The prostitute is the mother of what

---

1. Pelosi, "Remarks Upon Reconvening," para. 6.

disgusts God as she rides the beast drunk on the blood of those who have born witness about Jesus.

The vision is a complex picture. The woman is a model of beauty that lures people into union with her. From heaven's perspective, however, those entering her embrace commit spiritual adultery. Nevertheless, she rides a powerful beast and seduces the kings of the earth who will ultimately ally themselves against the Lamb and his followers (Rev 16:14–16; 17:2, 14).

3. Explaining the Symbols (Revelation 17:7–18)

As the angel speaking with John explained the vision to him, readers encounter as many questions as answers. True to apocalyptic form, the symbols—even when explained—are multifaceted.

The Beast

The beast's seven heads are identified both as hills and kings, or kingdoms. The seven hills point to Rome, which was situated on seven hills. Consequently, the kings may be emperors, but here we bump into a problem. If John wrote Revelation during Domitian's reign (81–96 BCE), the empire had experienced more than "five heads" that had come and gone by this point. In fact, Domitian was the twelfth emperor. Complicating the situation further is the statement that the beast itself is an eighth king (Rev 17:11), thereby raising the question of its relation to the seven heads.

One easily loses the forest among the trees of John's symbolism. Rome sat for the portrait of the beast, but the beast represents more than Rome. John's intent was not for his readers to spend our time trying to determine which emperor is "head number five." The numbers seven (heads) and ten (horns) symbolize the totality of the best's reign in opposition to God. He is the one who made war with the church (Rev 11:7) and who was behind the gathering of the kings to make war with the Lamb (16:13–16).

This beast also becomes a foil for God, which the angel implies. Whereas John repeatedly identifies God as the "one who was and who is and who is to come" (Rev. 1:4, 8; 11:17; 16:5), the beast is the one who "was and is not and is about to arise from the abyss to go to destruction" (17:8, author's translation). Despite all its asseverations about permanence and its faith in self-sufficiency, the beast rises only to proceed to its destruction.

This message offered hope and encouraged the suffering churches in places like Pergamum and Smyrna—hope that the end was in sight. The totality of evil would come to an end and the church's job was to avoid joining those awestruck by the beast (17:8). When people become seduced by the beast, they follow suit with the ten horns and transfer their loyalty to it. The horns represent client kings who did just that: they transferred their authority to the empire. As such, they gathered to wage war with the Lamb, but the Lamb's victory remains a foregone conclusion since he is the true Lord of lords and King of kings (Rev 17:14).

The Waters

The woman John saw sat on many waters (Rev 17:1), which the angel identified as peoples, crowds, nations, and tongues (Rev 17:15). That identification overlaps with the lists of people who rejected the church's testimony (11:9) and to whom John prophesied (10:11). Indeed, all three passages describe the same group.

These people join the ten kings and the beast in the unexpected destruction of the woman (Rev 17:16–17). The desolation, nakedness, and fire inflicted on the woman who symbolizes Rome—along with the consumption of her flesh—resembles the fate of cities and peoples that fell under God's judgment in the Old Testament (Jer 49:2; Ezek 16:37; 30:14; 39:18–20). The fact that some of the people regret the woman's destruction in Rev 19 suggests they too were deceived by evil when they allied themselves with the beast. They unwittingly sawed off the branch on which they sat.

The Woman

Revelation 17 closely associates the word "great" with the woman: she is "the great prostitute" (Rev 17:1) and "the great city that has dominion over the kings of the earth" (17:18 ESV). The tattoo on her forehead either labels her, "Babylon the great" (17:5). This greatness resonates with other passages that name Babylon "the great city" (Rev 16:19; 18:10–21). The repetitious annunciation of Babylon's greatness smacks of its hubris and need for more. Those who pursue greatness will never deem themselves sufficiently great. For Babylon—i.e., Rome—no amount of worldwide dominion would suffice. She would perpetually need her subjects to praise and affirm her majesty. In Revelation, such praise is appropriately directed to God, but significantly God is never described as "great."[2] For the one with true power and worth, there is no need to feign adoration.

In the Bible, Babylon became an archetype—a standard example—of the enemies of God and God's people. For that reason, first-century Christians would easily associate "Babylon" with Rome. Even so, the woman is larger than Rome. To an extent, she also resembles Jezebel from the Old Testament. Both were queens, adorned beautifully, accused of spiritual adultery, and both were destroyed along with their followers.

Jesus warned the church in Thyatira about following a prophetess cryptically identified as Jezebel (Rev 2:20). Thyatiran Christians were tempted into a way of life that accommodated Roman society and compromised their faith by associating with idolatrous practices. It is easy for Christians and churches to buy into a cultural worldview and to cover that worldview with spiritual sounding worlds. The spiritual beauty of that compromise however is no deeper and a glossy lacquer and it hoodwinks us into accepting the lie that insists we never compromised our sole fidelity to the Lamb by serving another.

We might also understand the spiritual threat of Babylon in terms of what the prostitute offers. She embodies a way of life propped up by the empire, whether Rome or any other empire. Her portrait resembles the goddess Roma—who personified Rome—because that was the empire known by John and his readers. The life offered by empire is made possible through a litany of abuses: economic, militaristic, religious, and so on. In Rome's case, she is drunk on the blood of the saints, but the propaganda she broadcasts enthralls even those in the church with her beauty and the life she offers in exchange for their cooperation.

The scary part of Rev 17 is not that the woman is some ancient or future empire that has arisen—or will arise—to persecute God's people. She certainly includes such ideas, but the terrifying part for modern Christians is the reality that she is much closer to home than we realize. We learn from Jesus' letter to Thyatira that she may very well be within the church where she seduces God's people to forsake the Lamb—or to get into bed with her

---

2. The times greatness is associated with God in Revelation, it describes God's action (Rev 15:3), an attribute of God (11:17; 21:3), or something else closely associated with God (6:17; 16:14; 20:11). This affirmation of the greatness of things associated with God highlights his greatness in a much more profound manner than simply affirming "God is great." By describing God's throne, or voice, or day as great, readers are left to conclude that however great we might imagine greatness to be, God himself far surpasses our imaginations.

when the Lamb isn't looking. Whatever name we give this rose—whether we call her Babylon, or Jezebel, or Rome—the scent remains the same: she constitutes a cultural and quasi-religious system goading people to indulge themselves in her embrace.

Her lure is her apparent permanence and the cultural and economic security she provides. Her rich ornaments suggest she can and does provide prosperity and security, perhaps even the religious security and freedom that Thyatiran Christians desired. The problem is that, like Seattle's Kingdome, *she's comin' down* and Rev 18 will provide a series of funeral dirges lamenting her downfall.

4. Responding to Babylon's Demise (Revelation 18:1-24)

As Revelation often does, chapter 18 presents two sides of an apocalyptic picture. Revelation 17 displayed the richly bedecked Babylon riding astride a great beast. She was a luring image of power and security. At the end of the chapter, the beast turned and consumed her (Rev 17:16). Revelation 18 now conveys another perspective as people respond in the aftermath of Lady Babylon's destruction.

Heaven Warns (Revelation 18:1-8)

The opening verses of Rev 18 look both to the future and present. It began with a mighty angel proclaiming that Babylon is already destroyed (18:1-3). The angel then elaborated the spiritual reality of the prostitute: she was a dwelling place for demons and a prison for unclean spirits, birds, and beasts (Rev 18:2).[3] Babylon's designation as a lair for demons and unclean animals illustrates Rome's spiritual depravity. The empire seduced nations to drink her wine, the kings of the earth committed prostitution with her, and she enriched the merchants of the earth with her powerful luxuries. Now, the angel proleptically claims this seductress is overthrown.

Revelation's readers, however, do not live in the aftermath of Babylon's downfall. For us, the prostitute's downfall is imminent and Rev 18:4-8 warns the church in the present. Revelation does not identify the origin of the voice calling the church out of Babylon. The speaker could be Christ in

---

3. Some English translations omit the beasts in v. 2 due to its absence in early Greek manuscripts.

v. 1, but it could just as well be an angel, or the one who sits on the throne. The call itself is by no means new. It reprises a common message from the prophets, particularly Jer 51:45 where God urged his people to leave Babylon in anticipation of her destruction (see also Isa 48:20; 52:11; Jer 50:8).

God's people embark on a spiritual exodus because God's judgment is immanent. Babylon's sins have piled up and God longs for his people to escape her fate (Rev 18:4–6). Meanwhile, the prostitute boasts that she sits as queen and will never encounter mourning. Such statements call to mind the Babylonian arrogance chided by Israel's prophets (Isa 47:7; Zeph 2:15). As with the first Babylon, newer instantiations of the empire fare no better when God removes sin.

God summoned his people out from Babylon's idolatrous practices. For Christians today, this is a spiritual as opposed to geographical move. There is no place or government to which Christians might flee and find refuge from sin. The Lamb is the only refuge. To depart Babylon is not to leave the city, but to resist the political, economic, and religious forces that render us complicit with the beast and his oppression of God's people. The church necessarily resides *in* the world, but must persevere in faith to avoid becoming one with the world. Revelation 18:4–8 addresses such Christians and calls them to repentance.

One's response to heaven's call out of Babylon will largely impact how one responds when God finally exacts punishment on Babylon. When the empire is overthrown, creation will respond in one of two ways: mourning or rejoicing.

Babylon's Clients Mourn (Revelation 18:9–24)

Following the warning about impending doom, readers encounter the first potential response to Babylon's demise: grief. It is the response of those empowered by Babylon. In this passage, Revelation draws from Ezekiel's long prophecy against Tyre, which also included laments. In the Old Testament, Tyre was an economic powerhouse whose destruction brought mourning to those it enriched (Ezek 26–27). Nevertheless, in its power, Tyre also became prideful and fancied itself divine (Ezek 28:1–10). God does not tolerate such competition. Those enriched by pompous kingdoms—whether Babylon or Tyre—will lament the destruction of such realms.

The Lament of the Rulers (Revelation 18:9–10)

The kings who lived luxuriously by colluding with the empire saw Babylon's smoke rising in the distance. Too scared to approach, they stood far off lest they share her torment. The rulers's lament employed the same language as the angel who addressed John in Rev 17 and thereby removes any doubt that this Babylon is "the great city" (18:10; cf. 17:18).

She prided herself on her royal status and denied the prospects of widowhood and mourning (18:7), but in one hour God's judgment arrived and rulers who prostituted themselves with her now mourned the demise of their mistress (18:10). Those empowered by a system of abuses cried out when that system collapsed. Following the removal of what once empowered the powerful, the earth's rulers become little more than mourners; their power was gone.

The Lament of the Merchants (Revelation 18:11–16)

Babylon's merchants comprised a second group of mourners. Their dirge followed a long catalogue of the various luxuries trafficked in the Roman Empire. It is a list of merchandise for which the empire's upper classes paid handsomely. With virtually no middle class in society, money became no object for those with wealth. As such, they could spend more than the annual income of a day-laborer on precious cargoes without thinking about it. In this economy, the merchants enriched themselves by leveraging society's economic inequality.

Even worse, the merchants became instruments of that abuse. The initial items on the list of cargoes—while extravagant—sound innocuous enough and the ability of Rome to provide them was one reason some saw the empire as praiseworthy. Even so, the conclusion to the list of cargoes was anything but innocuous. These merchants not only traded cinnamon, spice, and everything nice; they also trafficked slaves and human lives (18:13). The Greek puts things quite bluntly: they sold "bodies and souls of people" (author's translation). Rome's prosperity rested on reducing one fifth (or more) of its population to life as "living tools," which has led one scholar to describe its economy as parasitic.[4] From this vantage point, we hear Revelation indict Rome's entire economy as resting on a grim history of unrestrained profiteering.

---

4. DeSilva, *Discovering Revelation*, 43.

Now, however, the merchants—who grew their fortunes by selling everything from gold to spice to people—weep and mourn. God's rectification of evil becomes life shattering for those who profit from unrestrained consumption, inhumanity, and evil. No one remained to buy their lavish cargoes. In one hour, the merchants became unemployed. Like the rulers, they were reduced to mourning.

The Mariners (Revelation 18:17–19)

The final group to mourn Babylon's destruction were the seafarers. Like the merchants, they became the means by which Babylon (i.e., Rome) could transport its wares across the Mediterranean world.

Those who made their living by maritime transport cried out, "Woe!" along with the kings and merchants because Babylon was "laid waste" (Rev 18:19). A literal translation could be "she was made a desert," which further highlights the despair for those whose income derives from the sea. In keeping with mourning, the mariners cry out with ashes on their heads. Like their compatriots, they are now powerless.

Heaven Rejoices (Revelation 18:20–24)

Following the threefold lament of the rulers, merchants, and sailors, readers hear the jarring invitation to celebrate: "Rejoice over her, O Heaven! Also the saints and apostles and prophets, because God has exacted your judgment from her" (Rev 18:20, author's translation). Nothing between vv. 19–20 indicates an end of the sailors' lament, but it is unlikely the call to praise emanates from their lips. More probably, it originates with an angel (cf. 18:1, 21).

The call to praise erupts over the string of laments with the second potential response to God's judgment: rejoicing. The primary question is whether readers will respond to judgment with lamenting or rejoicing. Christians from Smyrna and Philadelphia would rejoice over Babylon's downfall. Conversely, Christians in Laodicea and Sardis who compromised their faithfulness probably found reasons to lament the idea of Rome's destruction. Economic collapse doesn't sound all that appealing to those enriched by the economy.

Meanwhile, Christians in Ephesus, Pergamum, and Thyatira found themselves somewhere in the middle. These were the churches Jesus addressed with both encouragements and warnings. They needed to choose repentance and follow the Lamb, which meant leaving behind the lure of Rome's long-standing empire.

The call to repent is one to heed quickly because of the downfall of the empire will occur violently and unexpectedly. This was illustrated by angel's symbolic act in Rev 18:21-24. The violent tossing of a millstone into the sea illustrated the abrupt downfall of Rome. No longer would the sounds of musicians or craftsmen or daily activities be found in it. Why such desolation? Because "by [Babylon's] sorcery all the nations were led astray and in [Babylon] were found the blood of the prophets and saints and all the slaughtered of the earth" (18:23c-24, author's translation). Babylon used its illustrious power to lead the world away from God and to persecute those who followed God. That way of life typically brings short term gains in terms of wealth and power, but in the long-term leaves people spiritually bankrupt and under God's judgment. That is the fate of Babylon and those who embrace her.

5. A Closer Look at Babylon

In Revelation 19, Babylon's fall will fade into the background, eclipsed by praise. But before proceeding, we must contemplate what Babylon represents. On one level, it depicts the Roman empire and its persecutions of early Christians. On another level, Rev 17-18 segues seamlessly into praise in chapter 19, followed by the wedding of the Lamb (19:7-10) and the final battle between Jesus and the beast (19:11-21), events that would seem to remain in the readers's future.

All of this raises the question: what is Babylon? The expansive description of Babylon's reach in Rev 18:3 ensures that she symbolizes much more than Nebuchadnezzar's kingdom in the Old Testament, or even Caesar's empire in the New Testament. Revelation says that *every nation* has drunk from her wine. Such words point the Christian's attention not only to godless foreign countries "over there," but to our own homes too. The power of the beast and Jezebel lurk close to Revelation's readers. No nation, and perhaps no ruler, can escape her temptation.

A faithful reading of Revelation follows Richard Bauckham's observation that "any society that fits Babylon's cap must wear it. Any society which absolutizes its own economic prosperity at the expense of others comes under Babylon's condemnation."[5] Babylon is the government and economic system that lures people away from the sacrificial lifestyle of the Lamb of Rev 5. As such, Babylon takes different forms in different periods of history. In Moses' life, Babylon took the form of Egypt. For Elijah, it was Samaria under King Ahab and Queen Jezebel. For Jonah, it was Nineveh. For Jesus, it was Jerusalem's religious establishment. For John and Paul, it was Rome. For Christians today, it might be Beijing; Brussels; Hollywood; Moscow; New York; Tehran; Washington, DC; etc.

The prominence of economic prosperity and power in Rev 17–18 should make American Christians a bit fidgety as we read the story. Frankly, it should make most Western Christians uncomfortable. Those who have taught Bible studies on Revelation outside the western hemisphere are at times surprised when students naturally connect Babylon with the United States. That is not a comfortable interpretation for us to hear and to be certain American Christians have plenty of rebuttals, at least I certainly do.

Nevertheless, we must ask ourselves whether we prefer a safe or faithful reading of Revelation. Safe readings of the book relegate Babylon to ancient history by speaking only about ancient Rome; or, they morph Revelation into a tabloid from the future that speaks about what will occur when some enigmatic and malevolent enemy arises who will certainly look more like the people we dislike than we ourselves. Both approaches render Revelation safe because it no longer addresses us in the here and now. A faithful reading is willing to ask, "Could I be one of the merchants?" "Am I one of the people who profits off—perhaps unknowingly—the injustice inflicted on others?" "Do I benefit from policies and economic choices that lead, or push, people away from the Lamb?"

A self-critical reading of Revelation is the best way to ensure one does not join the masses led astray by Babylon. John was clear: *no nation* escapes Babylon entirely (Rev 18:23) and that includes whichever nation the reader calls home. Our only escape is to follow the Lamb by living sacrificially like Jesus and by becoming the prophetic witness that identifies sin wherever it is found while calling people to repentance.

---

5. Bauckham, *Theology*, 156.

6. Jesus' Bride and Jesus' Victory (Revelation 19:1–21)

If set to music, one might expect Rev 18 would be played in a minor key with its focus on lamentation. By contrast, Rev 19 would ring out with the joyous tones of heavenly rejoicing in praise of God's judgment, glory, salvation, and power. Evil met its match and finally reached its end. That is why heaven resounds with a chorus of hallelujahs—a Hebrew expression meaning "praise the LORD."

Two primary metaphors emerge from Rev 19 that will guide our exploration of the chapter: the church as Jesus' bride and Jesus' judgment of evil as a military victory.

Jesus' Bride

Revelation 19:1–8 displays the book's remarkable ability to depict different aspects of one reality. At first, followers of Jesus appear as the martyrs, those whose blood God avenged (Rev 19:2). But before long, they reappear as a bride prepared for her husband (v. 7). As heaven resounded with hallelujahs, John heard the sound of a great crowd that roared like many waters and thunders (v. 6). This thunderous throng cried out, "Hallelujah! For the Lord God, the Almighty, reigns! Let us rejoice and let us be overjoyed and let us give glory to him because the wedding of the Lamb has come and his bride has prepared herself" (19:6–7, author's translation).

The wedding scene appropriates a prominent theme from the Old Testament that portrayed Israel as God's wife (Isa 54:4–8; 62:5; Jer 2:1–3; Ezek 16; 23). God had married Israel in the covenant at Mount Sinai, but she became unfaithful. She committed prostitution with other gods and nations. Nevertheless, God promised reconciliation. Revelation picks up that theme. Now that God has removed the source of adultery (Babylon), God's people found themselves ready for communion with him. That people, the church, now unites with Jesus as the bride of the Lamb (Rev 19:7–8).

As the bride, she has clothed herself in pure, fine linen (Rev 19:8). That description might recall Babylon the prostitute who also girded herself with linen (18:16). Babylon's linen, though, was never described as "pure"—some English versions say "clean"—because she was the source of impurity. Conversely, in Rev 19, the ones wearing pure linen are the saints—those persecuted by Babylon—who have washed their robes in the blood of the Lamb (7:14). Their fine garments symbolize their righteous actions (19:8).

As John saw this beautiful picture of the church's union with Christ, the angel leading him instructed him to write "blessed are the ones summoned to the wedding supper of the Lamb," and he was overcome and fell in worship at the angel's feet (19:9–10, author's translation). It is easy to allow ourselves to become distracted from Christ, but the angel was faithful to point John back to God by acknowledging that he was unworthy of worship. The angel was only a fellow servant alongside John and the church.

Jesus' Victory and Judgment

The second major metaphor running through Rev 19 portrays Jesus' judgment as a victory. Christian readings of the New Testament sometimes downplay God's judgment. We occasionally imagine this was something exacted only by that angry God in the Old Testament. Conversely, some Christians focus on God's judgment to the extent that it distorts the biblical picture of God such that divine anger eclipses all other attributes. The solution to such distortions is not to jettison a doctrine of divine judgment, but to correct it.

An appropriate starting place is the picture of the church discussed above. Christ's bride clothed herself with "righteous acts," which translates the Greek word *dikaiomata* (Rev 19:8). This word derives from the same root that lies behind the words "righteousness" and "justice" in English translations. Through righteous—or just—actions, the church was faithful to her husband—Christ—and for this she suffered. That suffering was a form of Babylon's *adikaiomata* (or, *in*justice) for which the prostitute stood condemned. God called the church out of Babylon because Babylon's sins generated the opposite of *dikaiomata* (18:4–5). Throughout the Scripture, God is in the business of establishing righteousness and justice and removing injustice. He is not an ogre fuming with anger; he is the creator who sets the world right (*dikaios*), which is why God's judgments are praised in Rev 19:2 as "true and just/righteous (*dikaiai*)."

God's judgment is restorative; it returns creation to a right relationship with God. We see that restorative intent throughout the latter chapters of Revelation: the four living creatures representing the animal world join in praise (Rev 19:4), the angel of the waters agrees God's judgment is just (16:5), and God makes all things new (21:1–2, 5). Since God seeks restoration, he has allowed ample opportunity for people to repent and has sent the church as a prophetic witness that calls the world back to the Lamb.

Revelation 19 celebrates God's justice as a successful military campaign against evil's recalcitrant injustice. Jesus arrived on the white horse as the one who is "faithful and true" (19:11–21). In truth, he has not come to fight, but to render a verdict against evil. His eyes are fiery as they were when we first encountered Jesus in Rev 1:14 and the fire here is likely associated with judgment. The fact that Jesus comes to judge suggests he already has claimed victory.

It is also noteworthy that even before the battle, Jesus' white garment is dipped in blood, a remnant of the blood he shed on the cross (19:13). Calvary is where the victory was won. Although that event looked like defeat, we now find Jesus victorious in God's campaign against evil.

When Jesus arrived for battle, he rode at the head of an army clothed in linen. This is the people of God standing with Jesus and wearing the white and pure garments worn by the church and martyrs (Rev 19:14; cf. 6:11; 19:8). This is the white-robed people comprised of every nation, tribe, people and language that stands before the throne and the Lamb (7:9); the people symbolized by the twenty-four elders clothed in white (4:4).

Before the final battle, an angel summoned the birds of the earth, inviting them to a great feast following the destruction of God's enemies. Kings, rulers, horses and their riders will become carrion. The invitation to the birds draws on Ezek 39, in which birds and beasts are summoned to pick through the bodies in the aftermath of God's victory over Gog and Magog. Revelation 19 refashioned those enemies as the beast and his cohorts whom God defeats in Christ. Whatever may take place physically in the future, the victory in Rev 19 includes a spiritual victory—the picture of birds feeding on corpses likely depicts the spiritual fate of those who resist Jesus' rule as King of kings and Lord of lords.

The battle itself is reported in Rev 19:19–21. In it, the beast and false prophet are defeated and cast into the lake of fire. Along with them went anyone who had received the beast's mark. Their fate became the same as the one with whom they chose to identify. The rest were killed with the sword from the mouth of the rider on the white horse.

This passage appears to narrate some kind of a future victory claimed by Jesus over a world united against him and his people (Rev 19:19). As such, it may report the same events as Rev 16:12–16 and 20:7–10. Be that as it may, readers should contemplate how different this final battle is from the one Christians typically imagine. I have sat through Sunday school lessons as old ladies of the church began to worry about the need to undergo some sort of military basic training to prepare for their part in the battle. One children's video depiction of Rev 19 portrays a literal battle between Jesus and the angels and Satan and his demons.

Significantly, Rev 19's battle report includes nothing of that sort. No fighting happens here; the battle was already won on the cross. The only weapon used in this passage is the sovereign word of Jesus, the sword of his mouth. His judgment proceeds as he renders a verdict against sin. This passage narrates Jesus' word striking the nations whom he shepherds with a rod of iron (19:15; cf. Ps 2:9; Rev 2:27; 12:5). Jesus is the Word of God (19:13; John 1:1–14) and God's word is powerful and effective. It is this word that spoke creation into existence in Gen 1 and now that same word speaks evil into the nonexistence of spiritual death. This is the self-chosen punishment for those who refuse Jesus' reign.

7. Woe or Hallelujah?

Revelation 17–19 covers a lot of territory. We began with the great prostitute and the lure of peace and prosperity Babylon offers the world. Next, John reported the prostitute's downfall through a chapter of laments cried out by her lovers. Finally, Rev 19 resounds with praise offered to God for Babylon's demise and for God's victory over evil and vindication of the saints.

This all raises the question of whether readers find themselves among those crying out "Woe!" or "Hallelujah!" at Babylon's demise. Put another way, will we be among those invited to the wedding supper of the Lamb (Rev 19:7–9), or among those who constitute the main course of the gruesome feast prepared for the birds (vv. 17–18)?

One accepts the invitation to the wedding of the Lamb by heeding the command of Christ, "Come out of her, my people" (18:4). That exodus is hard work. Babylon's embrace feels natural. The lure of her power and security and the comfort of her perceived permanence deceives people into following someone besides the Lamb.

No doubt, Christians in Laodicea and Sardis found the laments of Rev 18 troubling. Wealthy and comfortable churches heard a wealthy and comfortable society crying out in horror over Babylon's demise. The intent of Revelation was to awaken the sleeping church to realize its embrace of sin. The catalogues of Rome's cargoes and the abuses it inflicted on people were sins that had piled up to heaven and those who found themselves complicit with these sins experienced God's judgment.

Revelation 17–19 is convicting because it places a heavy focus on the economics of empires and therefore speaks not only to ancient Rome but also to future Romes. This passage also directly addresses Christians who benefit from such sinful societies. The self-critical question readers must ask is, "Do I prosper from sin?"

Answering that question yields profound implications for how believers live. Once one recognizes where he or she benefits from sin, it is time to repent. In my own life as a reader of Revelation, this changed how I save for retirement. Certain companies guarantee great profits in the stock market, but to invest in them is also to invest in policies and agendas that not only applaud sin but lead people into it. The question Revelation posed to me was whether such investments positioned me with the merchants of Rev 18?

Jesus' path is difficult to follow. But it is also one with hope. Despite the problems that plague our world, Revelation reveals that Jesus has won the victory and will one day remove all competing rulers and dominions. To stand behind Jesus with the glorified armies in Rev 19 requires leaving Babylon and following the Lamb. It requires the sacrifice modeled by Jesus' earthly life. In the midst of that life of sacrifice, we follow the Lamb and remember the words to Maltbie Babcock's hymn "This Is My Father's World":

> This is my Father's world
> O let me ne'er forget
> That tho' the wrong seems oft so strong,
> God is the Ruler yet.
> This is my Father's world.
> The battle is not done
> Jesus, who died, shall be satisfied,
> And earth and heav'n be one.[6]

---

6. Babcock, "This Is My Father's World."

For Further Study

Discussion Questions

1. How do you imagine different churches in Rev 2–3 might respond to the idea that *every* nation is in bed with the prostitute of Rev 17?
2. In Rev 18, several groups of people respond to the demise of Babylon. With which group do you most closely identify?
3. How might people ensure they will be among those who proclaim "Hallelujah!" when Jesus returns rather than "Woe!"?

12

Touring the New Creation

Preparatory Reading

- Revelation 20–22
- Ezekiel 38–39

1. Introduction

I have written quite a bit over the years, but it is not my favorite activity. Writing annoys me because thoughts that are clearly formed in my mind inevitably come out jumbled when typed. As clear as I might try to be in my writing, miscommunication always crops up somewhere along the line.

I suspect John would sympathize with me if he could read commentaries on Rev 20–22. He saw what he saw and perhaps knew exactly what he wanted to communicate about his visions. Nevertheless, over the centuries John's readers have taken the words he wrote and arrived at divergent—sometimes contradictory—understandings of what he meant.

Our purpose in this chapter is not to explore each of the interpretive possibilities. I will offer an interpretation of the text and say why I believe it resolves issues that others leave unaddressed, but *no* interpretation of Rev 20–22 is without difficulty. In any case, endlessly debating the different possibilities quickly becomes divisive and occludes the truth that is most important for John: Jesus has the victory, will make all things new, and invites his followers to live with him. That is where the focus should remain for readers of Revelation.

2. A Final Series of Visions (Revelation 20:1—22:5)

Revelation 20:1 launches a final series of four visions, each one beginning with the words "and I saw" (20:1, 4, 11; 21:1, author's translation). Because the final vision is much longer than the others, we will treat it in a separate section below. Here, our focus will be on the first three sights that John witnessed.

Vision 1: The Binding of Satan (20:1–3)

The initial verses of Rev 20 are among the most hotly contested in the Bible. The meaning and timing of the millennial binding of Satan—and the ensuing reign of the church—has generated much debate. A fresh look at the text is the best starting point for any analysis, so that is where we shall begin.

What John Saw in Revelation 20:1–3

John watched an angel descend from heaven with the key to the abyss. That opening image bears similarities to other places Revelation begins a new sequence of visions (Rev 10:1; 18:1). The key possessed by the angel indicates the authority delegated to him, as in Rev 9:1–3. In that passage, an angel unleashed evil by unlocking the shaft to the abyss; here, the abyss is locked so as to restrain the devil.

It is noteworthy that the angel in Rev 20 remained unnamed. Given the cosmic showdowns characteristic of apocalyptic writings—like the epic hero movies of our own time—we would expect one of the story's heroes to accomplish the task of capturing the supervillain. We might expect Michael or even Jesus to complete this task, but it is a nameless angel. The point speaks to God's sovereignty. The binding of Satan did not require Jesus fighting another battle or some über-angel exerting unprecedented power to arrest the enemy. Jesus has already won the victory—checkmate, game over. The binding of Satan is simply the tying up of loose ends and required zero pomp and circumstance. These verses are not the climax of Revelation.

Verse 2 attributes several names to Satan. He is "the dragon, the ancient serpent, who is the devil and Satan" (author's translation). Those names also appeared in Rev 12:9—another place the devil was cast down in defeat. In Rev 12, the life, death, and resurrection of Jesus brought about that defeat. The same holds true in Rev 20. These verses retell, or recapitulate, a story that we have already seen.

Some readers will justifiably object by appealing to experience: when we look around our world, it doesn't appear Satan is all that bound up following Jesus' resurrection. Nevertheless, even prior to the resurrection, Jesus implied he had bound up Satan (Matt 12:29). That is consistent with other passages that speak of the limiting of the devil's power (Luke 10:18; John 12:31; Heb 2:14). As such, readers should exercise caution against placing undue weight on experience when interpreting Revelation. The whole point of the book is to reveal what we cannot see based on our experience.

Revelation 20:1–3 offers another perspective of the same reality we saw in chapter 12: the defeat of Satan. Additional parallels between the two stories substantiate this point:

- Both stories depict Satan in conflict with angels (12:7, 9; 20:1–2).
- Both stories narrate Satan being cast down (12:9; 20:3).
- Following his defeat, Satan's influence is limited (implied by the victory song of 12:10–12; 20:3).

The connecting points between Rev 20:1–3 and 12:7–12, not to mention the other NT passages cited regarding the binding of Satan, imply that the events of Rev 20:3 do not render Satan powerless. He still creates problems, but his power is curtailed. He cannot stop the church from its mission, nor can he unite the nations and rulers of the world together in an attempt to destroy the church. That activity will happen only when he is loosed at the end of the church age (20:7–10), which Revelation has narrated in 19:19–21 (cf. 16:12–16). For now, Satan is sealed up—his power is limited.

Despite this limitation, the devil's influence continues through his proxies, as we observed in the aftermath of Rev 12. After being cast out of heaven, the dragon receded into the background as other beasts did his bidding. The same situation lies behind Rev 20. Satan resembles an imprisoned mob boss who feeds directions to his crime syndicate.

At this point, however, close readers of the text may well raise an objection: in the sequence of Rev 19–20, haven't the beasts already been defeated and thrown into the lake of fire (Rev 19:20)? We must now address the timeline and structure of Revelation.

Linear Sequence or Recapitulation?

Western Christians naturally read Rev 19–20 as a linear sequence that assumes one story leads directly into the next. Indeed, the introductory words "and I saw" in 20:1 can support that way of reading. However, Gregory Beal is correct that in Revelation such phrases also introduce sections that are concurrent rather than sequential (cf. 19:11, 17, 19).[1] In fact, when Revelation introduces a vision with "and I saw" followed by an angel descending from heaven with some kind of power, "it always introduces a vision either reverting to a time *before the preceding section* . . . or occurring *at the same time as the preceding section*" (cf. 10:1; 18:1).[2]

With this in mind, Rev 20:1–3 retells an earlier story from the book rather than continuing the timeline from where Rev 19 left off. We have already observed several instances where Revelation did not follow a linear sequence. The seal, bowl, and trumpet judgments told and retold the same story repeatedly. Likewise, we saw that the stories of the two witnesses (11:3), the woman's time hiding from the dragon (12:6), and the sea beast's authority (13:5) all retold the same three-and-a-half-year time span. Likewise, given that Rev 19 provided several visions that overlapped with regards to the timeline (19:11, 17, 19), it is unsurprising to find a similar overlap in chapter 20, especially when remembering that the chapter divisions were not John's creation.

Excursus: A Brief History of Interpretation

In twentieth-century North America, three primary schools of thought dominated the field of interpretation regarding the millennium. Each model had as many permutations as its adherents.

Prior to two world wars, the post-millennial school enjoyed popularity with its belief that the church would accomplish its mission of evangelizing the world, thereby issuing in a thousand-year

---

1. Beale, *Book of Revelation*, 974–76.
2. Beale and Campbell, *Revelation: A Shorter Commentary*, 422 (italics in the original).

reign, followed by the return of Christ (after—post—the millennium). That eschatology reflected the optimism generated by the American revivalist movements of the nineteenth century, as well as the faith liberal Protestantism placed in humanity's progress.

Following two world wars and during a seemingly interminable cold war, things appeared much less optimistic. In this environment, dispensational premillennialism gained ascendency and remains dominant among North American readers. It is the model popularized in Christian fiction about the end times (like the *Left Behind* series). It teaches that a rapture will occur followed by a tribulation after which Jesus will defeat evil in the battle of Rev 19. In this school of thought, Jesus returns prior to (pre-) the millennium.

The third school of thought might be called the "realized millennium," or "inaugurated" millennium. It identifies the thousand years with the age of the church. In this view, the number one thousand is symbolic as opposed to literal in pre- and post-millennial thought. This view is often labeled "amillennial," which is a misnomer because the prefix "a-" implies a denial of the millennium. Adherents to this position believe the millennium began with the resurrection of Jesus and continues until his return. During this time Satan is bound and unable to exert his full force.

Whichever model one favors, it is important to adopt a stance of humility. As Christians, we believe the Bible is inspired, but our faith contains no requirements on affirming the inspiration of an interpretation of the Scripture. The task of theology is the task of putting together the pieces, which involves weighing evidence in different ways. We undertake this task with humility because we recognize we have not seen what John saw and we are far from omniscient. What Christians must believe is that Jesus will return to judge the living and the dead. The timing of that return is the primary debatable issue in Rev 20:1–3 and it is lamentable that Christians can become so dogmatic about the timing that they part fellowship and split the body of Christ.

Vision 2: The Thousand Years and the Final Battle (Revelation 20:4–10)

John's second vision contains two scenes. In the first scene, the church—or some part of it—reigned with Christ on heavenly thrones (Rev 20:4–6). This scene is simultaneous with the previous vision of the millennium; the church reigned during the dragon's imprisonment. The second scene reports the loosing of Satan after the thousand years and his subsequent gathering of the nations in rebellion against God (vv. 7–10). The timing of this scene is difficult to pin down and depends on one's conclusions regarding the millennium (see the excursus above).

The Millennial Reign (Revelation 20:4–6)

A millennial reign of the church with Christ is a joyous thought. For disenfranchised Christians in places like Smyrna and Philadelphia, the prospect of sitting with Jesus and having authority to judge provided hope. Likewise, the text extends hope to Christians today in places like Somalia, Iran, and North Korea. These are places where Christians fit the description of the church in Rev 20:4—beheaded for their testimony about Jesus and the word of God.

A major question with this scene, though, is who precisely reigns alongside Jesus. A purely literal reading of the text excludes everyone except the specific martyrs who happened to experience beheading as their method of execution. In the Roman world, that was merciful form of execution, typically granted to Roman citizens. But is it only the beheaded martyrs who reign with Christ?

More important than the manner of death are John's additional descriptions of this group: they faithfully bore witness about Jesus and clung to God's message (cf. Rev 1:9; 12:11). Such characteristics precipitated the martyrdom of those we encountered in the fifth seal (6:9), who were told to wait until their number was complete. Indeed, the people we find in Rev 20:4 are those who have followed the Lamb wherever he goes, including to martyrdom (see Rev 14:4). Now, in Rev 20, they receive vindication.

It is unlikely John intended to limit the millennial reign to beheaded martyrs alone. Rather, the beheaded represent the larger group of the faithful who reign with Jesus. English speakers use similar linguistic devices today. When someone excited about her purchase of a new car exclaims,

"Check out my new wheels!" the point is not really to draw attention to the wheels alone, but to see the vehicle.

Similarly, the martyrs in Revelation stand for the entire church. John said the Christians of Rev 20:4 refused to worship the beast and receive his mark (Rev 20:4). That could be any faithful Christian, though it is noteworthy that John assumed nearly everyone who refused to worship the beast would become a martyr (Rev 13:15). The picture of God's people—not only martyrs—reigning with Christ corresponds to other parts of the Bible. The saints seated on thrones in heaven correspond to Dan 7:9–10, 18. Similarly, Eph 2:6 says Christians are seated already with Christ in the heavenly places because we have been raised up with Christ from death to life. As N. T. Wright remarked about that passage, "they aren't just sitting there doing nothing."[3] They are reigning with Jesus. Granted there are significant differences between Eph 2 and Rev 20, but the overall pictures they offer exhibit striking similarities.

Whether one sees the group in Rev 20:4–6 as literal beheaded martyrs, all martyrs, or the entire church, one should remain humble and avoid becoming dogmatic. Rev 20 is the only chapter in the Bible to mention the millennium as such and the only one to mention a two-stage resurrection, which makes it difficult to ascertain this text's relation to other passages within the canon of Scripture.

Like the identity of the group in Rev 20:4, the duration of its reign is also debated. Some understand it as a literal thousand years preceding Christ's return, or following his return. Be that as it may, numbers in Revelation are often figurative and the number one thousand is suspiciously large and round. While a literal reading is certainly viable, it is no less viable to conclude the thousand years symbolizes the completeness of Christ and the faithful's reign.

All things considered, the present writer favors a symbolic reading of the millennial reign, especially in light of Eph 2. That said, this reading possesses deficiencies if applied to the entire church age. For instance, it is difficult to understand the connection between the reign of Rev 20 and the anticipated—presumably, still-future—reward for the martyrs in the fifth seal (Rev 6:9–11). Relating those two passages is no easy matter if the millennium corresponds to the entire time frame between Christ's resurrection and return.

---

3. Wright, *Revelation for Everyone*, 180.

If such objections hold against a symbolic reading, it might suggest a model that refuses to map onto any of the traditional modes of interpreting Rev 20: perhaps, the millennial reign envisions a limited time frame that may or may not correspond to a literal thousand years. That time frame would not necessarily equate with the entire church age either. Regretfully, to say much more borders on speculation and must be reserved for another book.

Whatever the case regarding the millennium, the concluding words of Rev 20:6 remain unambiguous. Those who came to life in v. 4 need not fear the second death. Additionally, they received the description that elsewhere depicts the people of God at its best: priests and royalty (cf. Rev 1:6; 5:10). Together these facets of the church's identity recall God's intent for his people at the beginning of the Sinai narrative (Exod 19:6). Thus, whether this group symbolizes the entire faithful people of God, or a subset thereof, the point remains that they embody what God desires of his covenant people.

The Final Battle . . . Again (Revelation 20:7–10)

The second scene of John's vision reports the aftermath of the millennium. Consequently, the timing of these verses depends largely on one's interpretation of the millennium. If one equates the millennium with the thousand years following the battle of chapter 19, then this scene follows that thousand-year period. However, if the millennium is a less specific period of time corresponding to the age of the church—or a different time frame—then things become less tidy. If the martyrs already reign with Christ (or will reign at some point in the future), how does Rev 20:7–10 relate to 19:17–21?

There is substantial overlap between the two passages: both speak of the peoples gathering for the purpose of "the war" (Rev 19:19; 20:8), both note that the peoples were deceived (19:20; 20:8), the lake of fire appears in each passage as the punishment for demonic deceivers (19:20; 20:10), and both predict the utter destruction of those opposed to God (19:21; 20:9).

Given that the kings and their armies all perished in Rev 19, the reappearance of their nations to wage war in chapter 20 is perplexing. Revelation 20:7–10 apparently replays the final battle from chapter 19. Bolstering this view is the fact that both passages speak about "the war" (Rev 19:19; 20:8), though the definite article—"the"—does not always appear in English translations. "The war," refers to the eschatological war—a typical feature of apocalyptic literature—in which Jesus claims the ultimate victory.

Another important element of the relationship between Rev 20:7–10 and 19:17–21 is their mutual reliance on Ezek 38–39. Ezekiel pronounced oracles against "Gog of the land of Magog" (Ezek 38:2, author's translation). For him, Gog was a "chief prince" (vv. 2–3) and Magog was a land located in the distant north (v. 15) that allied itself with people from the south (Put and Cush) and east (Persia). Ezekiel foresaw those nations gathering to wage war against Israel while Israel's God defeated them with torrential rain, hailstones, fire, and brimstone, thereby revealing his greatness and holiness to the nations (38:22–23). The corpses of those armies were given as food for birds and animals as a great sacrificial feast (39:17–20).

Who or what Ezekiel meant by the terms Gog and Magog is highly debatable. Even in Ezekiel's time, the names apparently designated ambiguous enemies from the north, which is the direction from which most empires attacked Israel. By the time Revelation was written, the enigma of Gog and Magog had expanded to become a sort of archetypal representation of those allied against God and his people.

The nations, in Rev 19, reflect Gog and Magog in the Old Testament by becoming food for the birds (Rev 19:17–18). Revelation 20:7–10 likewise connects its armies to Gog and Magog both explicitly and by mentioning fire in the defeat of God's enemies (cf. Ezek 38:22; 39:6). However, unlike Ezekiel—where Gog is a person and Magog is a land—in Revelation the two expand to include every nation allied against God from the four corners of the earth (Rev 20:8). As in Rev 19, the battle ended before it began and God threw the demonic deceivers into the lake of fire (20:8–10).

To summarize, Rev 20:7–10 recapitulates the final war we saw in Rev 19. In each of those chapters, the war is narrated with the imagery of Ezekiel 38–39 in which God's enemies present themselves as united and originating from the north. In Revelation, those enemies are not a specific people or nation, but all the nations united against God's people—the church.

Why Release Satan?

Before proceeding, there remains a question regarding Satan's release from his prison (Rev 20:7). Why "must" this happen (Rev 20:3)? Surely, no one would complain if he remained locked up eternally. Regrettably, the why question is not one Revelation answers. Perhaps the release showed that neither Satan nor the nations changed during the thousand years. Some conclude the release was needed to test those born during millennium, but John says nothing to this effect and it is unclear why it would be required if those living during that period had already proved themselves faithful. Such readings leave us with God giving the faithful one last chance to be damned rather than the damned one last chance to be saved.

Whatever the rationale behind the divine plan, the central point of this scene remains clear: part of God's plan preceding the final judgment includes the unbinding of Satan to ally nations against God's people. Just when it appears the encampment of the faithful will face destruction, God will claim victory, will defeat the nations, and Satan will join his cohorts in the lake of fire. Like the first scene in Rev 20:4–6, this one offered hope to suffering Christians in Asia Minor and challenged comfortable Christians to follow the Lamb lest they find themselves among the hordes allied with Gog and Magog.

Vision 3: The Final Judgment (Revelation 20:11–15)

Just as Revelation narrated the last judgment from different angles in the earlier judgment cycles, we now receive a final depiction of that judgment, this time told from the angle of a heavenly court-scene. Like the other times God has appeared in Revelation, creation reacted in catastrophic ways. With the sixth seal, a massive earthquake struck the earth and the sky was "rolled up" (Rev 6:12–14); the seventh trumpet also brought a great earthquake (11:19); and with the seventh bowl, the earthquake caused islands and mountains to flee while the sky dropped hundred-pound hailstones (16:17–21). Likewise, in Rev 20:11 God's appearance in judgment caused the earth and sky (or, "heaven") to flee, but no place was found for them. Creation cannot escape its creator.

Next John witnessed the dead standing before the great white throne. These included all who were not already raised in Rev 20:5–6. In line with Paul's statement in 2 Cor 5:10, the people stood before the judgment seat of Christ to receive compensation for their deeds done in the body. The truly scary part of this judgment is that it is based on one's deeds as recorded in the opened record books (Rev 20:12).

That should engender fear for everyone. Whether we are from Smyrna or Sardis, the record of our actions cannot possibly acquit us before the great white throne. All have sinned and all have been unfaithful to the

Lamb, falling short of his glory. Regardless of how many good works the books might record for a given individual, they will also report that person's litany of failures and rebellions. If Rev 20 ended with v. 14, it would be the most troubling passage in the New Testament, if not the entire Bible.

Thanks be to God, then, that v. 15 supplies the good news that the judgment also factors in the contents of the Lamb's Book of Life. The Book of Life lists the names of people welcomed into the New Jerusalem (Rev 21:27). Even better, the roster of names has nothing to do with human merit because it was recorded before the foundation of the world (13:8; 17:8). The writing of one's name in the book is an act of grace. We cannot save or acquit ourselves before the judgment seat of Christ. But we do not need to do so because the Lamb has already written the names of his people in the book, died for them, and risen again so that they escape the second death. This is grace: the inscription of one's name in the Book of Life is entirely an unearned gift from God.

Let the reader be warned, though: although we can do nothing to inscribe our names in the book—we simply receive God's gift—we also need to remember that Revelation offers no free passes. Confidence that my name is written in the Book of Life does not grant license to sin so that God's grace may abound in spite of my unchristlike character. Jesus made this point to the church in Sardis when he implied the possibility of erasure of names from the Book of Life (Rev 3:5). That is the consequence of persistent refusal to follow the Lamb. Although we cannot write our names in the book, our willful choice to rebel against Christ—to choose unfaithfulness—is a choice to remain in spiritual death instead of receiving the life of the Lamb. That is a choice Jesus permits us to make and if we persist in it he will in the end honor our choice by erasing the names of those he died to save.

John witnessed those whose names were omitted from the Book of Life being cast along with Death and Hades into the lake of fire. This is the eternal abode of the dragon and the beasts and is a place of torment (Rev 20:10, 13–15). Christians have different opinions on the reality of hell. Some question whether it even exists; others ask whether its fire is symbolic or literal. The word "hell" itself never appears in Revelation and the lake of fire may well be symbolic. Even so, the symbols of Revelation correspond to reality on one level or another. Revelation does not elaborate on the lake of fire other than to say it is a place of torment (20:10), which suggests a place of conscious suffering.

Whatever the lake may be, Revelation is unambiguous: this is a place people want to avoid. Many ancient Christian writings speculated about what befalls different kinds of sinners in hell, but Revelation's position is that no elaboration is necessary. The juxtaposition of eternal suffering with the invitation to enter Christ's loving salvation should be enough information for us.

Some look at God's judgment from the angle of punishment and conclude God is an evil despot who looks for reasons to smite sinners. That, however, is not the picture of divine judgment one finds in Revelation. Miroslav Volf summarized the situation well:

> God will judge, not because God gives people what they deserve, but because some people refuse to receive what no one deserves; if evildoers experience God's terror, it will not be because they have done evil, but because they have resisted to the end the powerful lure of the open arms of the crucified Messiah.[4]

Significantly, Revelation does not end with God's judgment. This is not John's final vision. The final word in Revelation involves life with God and it is to this topic that the next vision turns.

3. The Final Vision (Revelation 21:1—22:5)

John's final vision in Revelation surveys the New Jerusalem situated within a new cosmos. For many, this passage represents a—perhaps the—primary picture of heaven in Scripture. Here we find the streets of gold, life without tears, and gemstones in abundance. As one might unexpectedly find beauty cracking open a geode, John's final vision has treasure to reveal. One unexpected discovery is learning the new creation is not somewhere that Jesus takes us; it is something that he brings with him. Additionally, the New Jerusalem that we so quickly associate with God's dwelling place also appears as a people, "the bride of the Lamb." What might these points suggest?

Because the text is so interconnected within itself, and because of its frequent use of the Old Testament, it will be helpful to organize our discussion by the predominant themes in the vision rather than by proceeding verse by verse.

---

4. Volf, *Exclusion and Embrace*, 298.

New Creation

Perhaps the greatest discrepancy between New Testament theology and popular Christian imagination about the return of Christ is our belief that "heaven" is somewhere we go. Certainly, heaven is the place God abides and we have communion with him there (Eph 2:6; Phil 3:20; Heb 12:22–24). Nevertheless, the final picture the Bible leaves for the church to ponder is not one of escape from a dysfunctional world by flying off to paradise. That would constitute a divine surrender of the old creation to brokenness. Instead, resting on God's victory over brokenness, Rev 21–22 reveals the arrival of a new heaven and new earth saturated with God's presence.

Such a hope hardly begins with Revelation. God had already promised a new heaven and earth in Isaiah (Isa 65:17). The problem with the old heaven and earth was that, while God had created them and deemed them "good," they also became marred by sin. That marring was not only earthly but also heavenly. The book of Hebrews taught Jesus' atonement differed from Israel's sacrifices since Jesus entered heaven itself to effect atonement, not the earthly replica of God's dwelling (the temple). In other words, Jesus' atonement removed sin in heaven itself. Along with this, N. T. Wright observed that Revelation has spoken of war in heaven.[5] The effects of sin reach further than Christians typically imagine. Heaven and earth require remaking and this is the work God unveiled in Rev 21:1–2.

The New Creation's Population

This new creation includes a larger group of people than we might expect. Many of us may be surprised by who we find in the new creation and who we do not find there. Unsurprising inhabitants of the new creation are God's people, the bride of the Lamb (Rev 21:9). These are the ones who worship God and the Lamb, see his face, and bear his name (22:3–4). They drink from the water of life and enjoy a relationship with God as his children (21:6–7). Revelation symbolized this people—as before—by combining two images from the Bible: the twelve tribes of Israel and the twelve apostles (21:12–14; cf. 4:4).

Also unsurprising to many readers, especially given the story of Rev 19–20, are certain exclusions from the new creation. Those left out are the

---

5. Wright, *Revelation for Everyone*, 188; see also Rev 12:7.

unfaithful, idolaters, and so on (Rev 21:8). The new creation is without sin; the former things passed away.

That is what is unsurprising about the new creation's population. What *is* surprising might be the inclusion of kings who bring the glory of the nations as tribute to God (Rev 21:24–26) and the nations themselves (21:24; 22:2). Given the destruction of the nations earlier in Revelation and the fact that the kings seemed to be the ones leading the nations away from God, it is surprising to find them included here. Perhaps this cautions us against taking the earlier visions too literally. Even as nations align against God, some may resist the temptation to embrace the beast. Such resistance affords the opportunity to find a place in God's new creation and to receive healing there (22:2).

The inhabitants of the new creation are a holy people; free from sin and living in God's presence. In both the Old and New Testaments, proximity to God renders one holy. We are holy as we walk with the Holy One. In the Old Testament, holy people and items were set apart for use in worship and service to God. That is exactly what we find in John's vision. Those occupying the new creation see God's face (proximity), have his name on their foreheads (set apart), and serve him (i.e., they are employed in worship; Rev 22:3–4). They are holy.

Conversely, those excluded are the opposite of holy: the profane (21:27). The Greek word *koinos* in Rev 21:27 is sometimes translated into English as "unclean" (NASB, NRSV). But *koinos* is not the typical word for "unclean" in the New Testament. Rather, it designates what is "common, profane" in contrast to what is holy or clean (cf. Mark 7:2; Acts 10:14; 11:8). In Leviticus, the antithesis to holiness is that which is profane (Lev 10:10). Along these lines, Ezekiel also witnessed a wall separating the holy from the common in his vision of God's temple (Ezek 42:20). John's vision reflects the Old Testament's theology of holiness in that the holy and the common cannot coexist. Those near God in the new creation are holy, serve him, and see his face. Conversely, everything common (*koinos*) is excluded from the holy domain of God and his people in New Jerusalem (21:27).

This accounts for what may be surprising omissions among the new creation's inhabitants. John said that the cowardly and unfaithful found themselves in the lake of fire along with other sinners (21:8). Those groups probably include Christians from places like Sardis and Laodicea, as well as many of the other churches in Rev 2–3. These are Christians who failed to heed Jesus' warnings and to whom he will say, "I never knew you." They did not overcome by reclaiming their faithfulness to Christ alone. Instead, they forfeited their place in the new creation.

This survey of the inhabitants of the new creation exhibits—again—Revelation's ability to address multiple audiences. For those afraid to identify with Jesus or who compromise their loyalty to him, Revelation says we will be excluded from everything we find in chapters 21–22. Conversely, by remaining faithful to Jesus—or by repenting and reclaiming our faithfulness—Revelation offers the hope of holiness and eternity with the savior.

The World of the New Creation

Excluding New Jerusalem itself (see below) the new earth displays several remarkable features. The first thing you or I might notice in this new world is the lack of the sun or moon because God's glory provides its illumination (Rev 21:23). Scripture closely associates God and God's dwelling with "unapproachable light" (1 Tim 6:16; cf. Ps 104:2; Jas 1:17; 1 John 1:5). In the new creation, that light of God's presence emanates from Jesus so that the nations walk by God's light (Rev 21:23–24).

Also missing from the new creation is the sea (Rev 21:1). As one who loves the ocean, this has always been my least favorite statement in Revelation. Most interpreters detect here a theme that associates the sea with chaos and evil. If that is correct, the point of Revelation is that chaos and evil find no place in the new creation. While that may be a valid point, recent scholars have demonstrated problems with too quickly connecting the sea to evil. For starters, it too is part of God's good—old—creation (Gen 1:10; Ps 95:5).

A more nuanced reading is preferable. Chaos erupts as human and nonhuman creation devolves from the order established by its creator. The sea, as an entity in Scripture, often refuses to follow God's order. Though at times it can be calm and glassy (Rev 4:6), has a place in God's presence (1 Kgs 7:23–26; see our discussion of the sea in Rev 4:6), and even praises God with the rest of creation (Ps 96:11–13), the sea also poses a threat (Ps 74:13; 89:9), is something God conquers for the salvation of his people (Hab 3:8–15), and is the source of the enemy of God's people (Rev 13:1). These examples demonstrate a propensity to reject God's rule. If so, then exclusion of the sea in Rev 21:1 exemplifies how God's new creation includes not only a holy people that submits to God's will, but a holy landscape as well. What rebels against God is excluded.

Though lacking an ocean, the new creation does have a water source: its inhabitants drink from the spring of the water of life (Rev 21:6). Readers familiar with John 4 might hear an echo of Jesus' promise to the Samaritan woman and recognize the living water as an image for eternal life with God. As in John 4, the living water in Revelation originated with God and it flowed from God's throne (22:1). That glimpse of water flowing from God's presence also appeared in Ezekiel when the prophet saw a river of life flowing out of the temple that made seawater fresh and gave life wherever if flowed (Ezek 47:1–12).

Unlike the sea, this river of life furthers God's life-giving intent. Growing on either side of the river is the tree of life that bears twelve kinds of fruit year-round (Rev 22:2). The notion of one tree bearing different fruits sounds confusing and is likely an example of modern readers becoming too focused on details at the expense of the overall picture. More important for John is the fulfillment of Jesus' promise to provide access to the tree of life (Rev 2:7). John adapted Ezekiel's vision of the temple, by reducing the number of trees to one. Perhaps he saw multiple trees, but he mentioned only one in order to create an additional allusion to the tree of life in Genesis (Gen 2:9).

The tree of life bookends the Bible: it appeared in the garden of Eden and reappears in the new creation. Taking that cue to read Rev 21–22 alongside Gen 1–2, additional parallels emerge. Scholars familiar with the ancient Near Eastern background of Gen 1–2 identify a temple theology in that text. In Gen 1–2, creation became God's dwelling place, his temple.[6] Likewise, the garden of Eden resembled the gardens that adjoined sacred locations in the ancient world.

As in Gen 1–2, the Bible's closing chapters teach that creation will again become God's dwelling place. Additional parallels between Genesis and Revelation confirm this point. Besides the presence of the tree of life, life-giving water appears in both texts (Rev 22:1; cf. Gen 2:10–14; Ezek 47:1–12). Furthermore, as in the Bible's opening chapters, the new creation possessed no temple because God and the Lamb fill that role (Rev 21:22). God's dwelling is no longer localized within an earthly sanctuary; earth is the sanctuary where God meets his people (Rev 21:3). In this new creation, God's servants approach the throne to worship him. They no longer require protection from his presence. Rather, they see God's face (22:3–4).

---

6. One accessible articulation of this position is Walton, *Lost World of Genesis One*, 71–85. See also Morales, *Who Shall Ascend*, 39–53.

The picture of the new creation in Rev 21–22 is a picture of communion with God. God reclaimed what was lost in Gen 3. Tears were wiped away, the curse was no more, and isolation from God gave way to intimacy as the bride made ready for her husband.

The New Jerusalem

New Jerusalem is the focal point of the new creation in Rev 21:1–22:5. Although God inhabits the entire new heaven and new earth, his presence is especially manifested in the temple-city where we find the throne of God and the Lamb (Rev 21:2–3) and where the kings of the nations bring their tribute (21:23–24).

The pictures of God's throne, of nations bringing tribute, and of gates and foundations all suggest that the New Jerusalem is a place. Indeed, it is *the place* where God abides most fully. While Revelation points readers in this direction, it also complicates this reading by suggesting New Jerusalem is a people. Most explicitly, we see this when the angel invited John to come and see "the bride, the wife of the Lamb" (21:9; see also v. 2). This connection between Revelation's temple city and God's people furthers with the New Testament's teaching that God's people are his temple (1 Cor 3:16–17; 6:19; Eph 2:19–22; Rev 3:12).

So, is New Jerusalem a place or a people? John may have answered "yes." The symbolism resists "either/or" thinking. New Jerusalem is a place where God dwells, but like Jesus' teaching about the kingdom of heaven, it is not limited to a geographical realm. In any case, geography is not what makes it special. What makes it special is the God who inhabits his people.

Gemstones, Foundations, and Gates

John described a visually stunning city. Laid out as a giant cube with a wall, New Jerusalem was constructed of pure gold, as were its streets. The wall had twelve foundations, each one decorated with a different gemstone, and its gates were pearls.

The gemstones incorporated into the city's construction were radiant. In fact, the city as a whole had a brilliance like crystal-clear jasper (Rev 21:11 NASB). The word translated "jasper" could be nearly any shiny stone. Its appearance may have resembled a diamond that refracts light. In New

Jerusalem, this radiance is a visible manifestation of God's glory and presence, as it is in other apocalyptic writings.[7]

Setting aside the glory of God radiating from the city, the first architectural feature encountered by pedestrians entering New Jerusalem was its wall, which would appear puny in comparison to the city's height: the wall measured a little over two hundred feet high whereas the city was laid out as a 1,500-mile cube. The presence of the wall does not imply the threat of evil since those who create evil find themselves excluded from the new creation. Nevertheless, ancient readers considered walls a normal part of any important city's architecture. If it represents anything, Beale may be on track by suggesting the wall picturizes "the inviolable nature of the city's . . . fellowship with God."[8] In New Jerusalem, nothing can hamper one's communion with God.

The wall rested on twelve foundations fashioned from gemstones (Rev 21:19–20). Some overlap exists between the stones mentioned here and those of the high priest's breastplate in Exod 28:17–20. Nevertheless, Revelation's sequence of stones is apparently random and replaces some stones from Exodus with others. Thus, it is difficult to conclude John drew from Exodus directly at this point. If he did, it could reiterate the point that God's people are a kingdom of priests (see Rev 1:6; 5:10; 20:6).

As elsewhere in Revelation, God's people are symbolized through the combination of the apostles and tribes of Israel. Revelation associates the jeweled foundations of the city with the apostles and thereby implies the city is not solely a location, but also a people. Specifically, it is the people who receive and accept the proclamation of the gospel through the foundational teaching of the apostles.[9] Moving up from the foundation of New Jerusalem's wall, we find Israel's twelve tribes at the city's open gates.

Whether there is any specific significance behind the gates depicted as large pearls remains unclear. Perhaps this is one way John portrays the glamor of New Jerusalem over against the great prostitute of Babylon, who also bedecked herself with pearls (Rev 17:4). In any case, more important than the composition of these gates is what they do: they remain open—everyone in the new creation has access to God.

---

7. Mounce, *Revelation*, 390.

8. Beale and Campbell, *Revelation: A Shorter Commentary*, 479.

9. John Wesley explained the symbolism by concluding that the twelve foundations illustrate that "the inhabitants of the city had built on the faith which the apostles once delivered to the saints." See Wesley, *Notes*, 1044.

The twelve gates remind us of the ones observed by Ezekiel in his vision of God's temple city (Ezek 48:30–35). Both Revelation and Ezekiel associate the gates with the tribes of Israel. The entry point to life with God is found among his people. In the Old Testament, to live with the LORD, one had to enter through one of the tribes. In Christ, the foundational teachings of the apostles reveal Jesus' expansion of God's people to include the gentiles.

In Eph 2:11–22, Paul emphasized that Jesus brought the gentiles to God and made them and Jews into God's one people. That people, like New Jerusalem's wall, rests on a foundation: the apostles and prophets. In that foundation, Jesus functions as the cornerstone (Eph 2:20). Paul then continued that building metaphor and proclaimed that this diverse people is built together into God's holy temple.

In Rev 21:9–27, the tour of New Jerusalem makes a similar point to what Paul taught the Ephesians: God dwells among his people. Recalling Ezekiel's vision, John brings us to the place where God dwells, but unlike in Ezekiel, when we enter the city we find that there is no temple. Why? Because "God the Almighty—and the Lamb—is the temple" (Rev 21:22, author's translation). Consequently, New Jerusalem in which God abides has less to do with "where" than it does with "who." In New Jerusalem, God dwells among his people, the bride of the Lamb. That people becomes the city to which the world can look and say, "The LORD is there" (cf. Ezek 48:35).

The Bride and Her Measurements

When I was a child—and even a young man—I was oblivious to the many decisions that go into planning a wedding. It wasn't until I had a college course training me to do premarital counseling that I realized weddings have colors besides the bride's white dress. Another foreign concept for me was the practice of getting one's measurements. My world had been rather off the rack.

As with most western brides, the one in Rev 21:15–17 got measured. The angel ushering John throughout New Jerusalem held a golden measuring rod just as John himself had held a measuring rod in Rev 11:1–2. However, there is a significant difference between Rev 11 and 21. When John measured the temple, he was commanded to exclude its courtyard. In Rev 21, the measurer omits nothing.

The meaning of the city's dimensions in Revelation is debated. Twelve thousand stadia is roughly 1,400–1,500 miles, depending on one's Bible translation (see NASB, CEB, NIV, NRSV). A straight line between Rome and Jerusalem is nearly 1,400 miles so the size of the city would be a cube that is somewhat larger than that distance. For reference, the square mileage of New Jerusalem's ground level (2,250,000 square miles) is over one-third larger than the European Union (1,634,469 square miles) and over eight times larger than the state of Texas (268,597 square miles).

All that being said, John's point is not about making size comparisons but to show that trying to make comparisons is pointless. More significant than the precise measurement is the shape of the city: it is a cube, just like the temple's most holy place was (1 Kgs 6:20; Ezek 41:4). However, the city possesses no sanctuary, because the Lamb is the temple and God's presence is no longer localized in buildings. In Revelation, that inner sanctum reserved for God's presence enlarges to the size of a continent.

It is at this point that we should remember the city is also the bride. Her enormous measurements (twelve multiplied by one thousand and cubed) suggest she encompasses the entire people of God. Twelve is a symbolic way of envisaging God's people and one thousand is a figure of completeness. That complete people, spoken of in the Old Testament as outnumbering the grains of sand by the sea and the stars in the sky, occupies the landscape of the new creation and mediates God's presence. It is here that we encounter the truth proclaimed by the psalmist:

> LORD, our Lord,
> How majestic is Your name in all the earth,
> You who have displayed Your splendor about the heavens! (Ps 8:1)

4. The Epilogue (Revelation 22:6–21)

The final paragraphs of Rev 22 constitute an epilogue that includes several speakers. There is a sort of antiphony that echoes between Jesus; John, who is both the narrator and a character in the story; the angel, who has been accompanying him; and the church. As each entity speaks its final words for the book, many of the themes of Revelation draw together. Because the passage is so dialogical, it may help us to consider what each entity says in turn.

John's Last Words

The first and last speaker in Rev 22:6–21 is John. As the narrator of the passage, he fills in the gaps between any dialogue. In v. 8, John addresses his readers saying that he himself heard and saw what Revelation has reported. This verse also has an implicit warning for readers in that—for a second time—John mentions his temptation to worship the angel showing him these things. The faithful must remain vigilant to ensure that their worship does not deflect off of God onto another.

John addressed the readers again in Rev 22:18–19. This time, the address comes in the form of a warning for anyone who might add to or remove from the words of prophecy contained in Revelation. This is where things get challenging. For many readers of Scripture there is a very large discrepancy between the book we want to read and the book that we have in front of us. In the case of Revelation, the book people often desire is one that assures them of escape from trials and persecution. Or, other readers want a book that guarantees universal salvation for everyone, regardless of their acceptance of Christ. A faithful reading of Revelation leaves both parties deeply unsatisfied.

Revelation challenges its readers. Recognizing the temptation to amend the parts of Scripture that do not fit our predetermined desires, John offers a warning. The temptation to hear only part of Revelation, or to blunt its point with additional words and caveats that run contrary to its intent, dulls our ears to its ringing call to faithfulness, endurance, and repentance.

John's final words conclude the Bible with blessing: "*The grace of the Lord Jesus be with all*" (Rev 22:21). Different translations render the final words of the Bible differently because different Greek manuscripts contain different words. Some say, "the grace of the Lord Jesus Christ be with all the saints" (author's translation). Other manuscripts append the word "amen" as a fitting conclusion to the book. The earliest and best manuscripts exhibit the shorter reading reflected in the NASB: "The grace of the Lord Jesus be with all." Regardless of the specific Greek words, the intent of each of the versions is the same: John desires God's grace to become active in the lives of God's people.

Last Words from John's Guide

As the vision that spanned Rev 21:1—22:5 concludes, the angel who guided John's tour of New Jerusalem declared "these words are faithful and true" (Rev 22:6). That phrase duplicates the words of the one sitting on the throne in 21:5. The angel clarifies that God is the source of the revelation John received: God had sent the angel to show John what must soon happen; John in turn tells the church (22:6, 16). This was the precise pattern we saw in Revelation 1:1—Jesus sent a message through an angel to John for the church.

The angel specified that what he showed John would happen soon (Rev 21:6). This theme of the prophecy reaching its fulfillment in the near future is echoed in Jesus' words (22:7, 20) and in the angel's statement that the time is near (v. 10), as well as other parts of Revelation (cf. 1:1; 2:16; 3:11; 11:14). This soon-coming fulfillment is why Revelation speaks to the church of now—whenever "now" might be—as opposed to only the church of the "end times." What John recorded in Revelation applies now.

The angel also had the job of pointing John to Christ when John succumbed to the temptation of worshiping the angel (22:9). The angel's rebuttal resembled that of Rev 19:10: he is only a fellow servant with John, the prophets, and all who obey the words of Revelation. Those exhibiting such obedience will appropriately direct their worship to God, as the angel instructed John.

The angel's final statement instructed John not to conceal the prophetic words of Revelation (Rev 22:10–11). The time is near so the church needs to understand the message now. But the angel also recognized that some will refuse to hear and obey the message, so he concluded, "Let the wrong-doer still do wrong, let the unclean still be unclean, let the righteous one still perform righteousness, and let the holy one still be holy" (Rev 22:11, author's translation). God's people are to be faithful to their identity as doers of righteousness and as God's holy people. Such faithfulness constitutes a prophetic witness resembling that of Ezekiel to whom God said some would listen while others refused to hear (Ezek 3:27). Regardless of how one's faithfulness is received by others, God's people must exemplify the righteousness and holiness that life with him entails.

Jesus' Final Words

As in a few other places (besides Rev 2–3), Jesus himself utters a couple of interjections. In these, he also lists different titles for himself that we have encountered throughout in Revelation: he is the Alpha and Omega (Rev 22:13; 1:8), the first and the last (22:13; 1:17; 2:8; cf. Isa 44:6), and the beginning and the end (22:13; 21:6). Such statements speak to Jesus' divinity. As the church has confessed through the ages, he is the eternal Word, the uncreated Son of God. Jesus' titles also adopt the language of the Old Testament in 22:16: he is the root and descendant of David (see Isa 11:1, 10; Rev 5:5). That designation means that Jesus is not only the divine Son of God, he is the Messiah, Israel's deliverer descended from David. Next, Jesus identified himself as the bright morning star (22:16; cf. 2:28), which may connect to the Gospel of John's statement that Jesus is the light of the world (John 1:9; 8:12; cf. 1 John 2:8). Revelation 22:20 also identifies Jesus as the "one who witnesses" (author's translation; some Bibles translate this as "testifies" [NIV, NASB]; see also Rev 3:14). He is the witness to whom the Father gave the revelation that was transmitted by an angel to John (Rev 1:1; 22:16).

For those who follow him, Jesus promised a reward while highlighting the divide between the faithful and unfaithful (Rev 22:14–15).[10] He blessed those who washed their robes, recalling the great multitude of people in Rev 7:14. These are the faithful who enter New Jerusalem and receive access to the tree of life. In contrast, outside one finds those excluded from the new creation. They are called "dogs," which carried a very negative connotation in the New Testament. These are the sorcerers, sexually immoral, adulterers, and idolaters—those who refused to follow Jesus. We also find outside those who love and practice "lying." This may be simply another sin that indicates sinners of all types are excluded, but the larger context of Revelation suggests a different possibility. The false, or liars, are repeatedly identified as those who present themselves as faithful when in fact Jesus evaluates their works differently (Rev 2:2; 3:9). These are distinguished from the true church in whose mouth was found no lie (14:5).

Three times in this passage, Jesus says "I am coming quickly" (Rev 22:7, 12, 20), echoing what he proclaimed elsewhere in Revelation (2:16; 3:11). The repetition creates a refrain that returns us to the appropriate

---

10. Some interpreters do not agree Rev 22:14–15 was spoken by Jesus, though there is nothing to suggest he stopped speaking at the end of v. 13.

focus: Jesus is coming and we must remain faithful. Those who are faithful, reap the blessing that Jesus uttered for those who obey the words of Revelation's prophecy (22:7).

On one level, this is wonderfully encouraging. Sowing faithfulness reaps blessing. On the other hand, obedience to Revelation's prophetic words most often entails a very countercultural life. It is a life that must identify the idols of one's culture—idols in whose embrace the faithful may well have indulged themselves. Leaving culture's embrace for the savior becomes exceedingly painful, which is why Jesus said in the Gospels that the road to life is narrow.

The Church and Spirit

The final speakers we must mention appear in Rev 22:17. John says the "Spirit and bride say, 'Come!'" These words return us to the predominant theme of Revelation: worship. The bride of Christ and the Holy Spirit beckon his arrival, just as John does in v. 20—"Come, Lord Jesus." Likewise, the one who truly hears the words of Revelation exclaims, "Come!" In response, John also invites those who are thirsty to come and receive living water. As a thirsty people, we also say with the church, "Come!"

5. Conclusion

Revelation concludes with a marvelous picture of God abiding with his people. It is a reclamation of what creation lost in Gen 3. Once sin is undone and evil is rooted out, Jesus makes all things new. There is a new creation as well as a new temple city. The picture offered contrasts sharply with the lived experience of Christians throughout the centuries. The new creation is a place without pain and in which God wipes tears away from the eyes of his people (Rev 21:4). Such hopes encourage Christians whose lives are keynoted by mourning, crying, and pain despite their faithfulness.

These faithful ones gain entrance into New Jerusalem. They find themselves incorporated within the bride of Christ. As that bride, the church today already enjoys communion with Christ even as we now—with the church of Revelation—await the coming of the bridegroom. With that expectation, we might close our study with the words of Scripture and a hymn of the church:

Listen! My Beloved!
Behold, he is coming,
Leaping on the mountains,
Jumping on the hills!
My beloved is like a gazelle or a young stag.
Behold, he is standing behind our wall,
He is looking through the windows,
He is peering through the lattice.

My beloved responded and said to me,
"Arise, my darling, my beautiful one,
And come along.
For behold, the winter is past,
The rain is over and gone.
The blossoms have already appeared in the land;
The time has arrived for pruning the vines,
And the voice of the turtledove has been heard in our land.
The fig tree has ripened its fruit
And the vines in blossom have given forth their fragrance.
Arise, my darling, my beautiful one,
And come along!"
(Song 2:8–13)

"Called unto holiness," Bride of the Lamb,
Waiting the Bridegroom's returning again;
Lift up your heads, for the day draweth near
When in His beauty the King shall appear.[11]

---

11. Morris, "Called Unto Holiness."

13

Epilogue

Connecting Some Dots

I never enjoyed puzzles. As a child, I hated them and they still increase my blood pressure. The closest I ever came to enjoying a puzzle was preschool connect-the-dots exercises—those I can handle.

Having concluded our study of Revelation, there are several "dots" that have repeatedly popped out in the Scripture that we may now connect: alternate apocalyptic perspectives, the call to a new exodus, and faithful worship.

1. The Importance of Apocalyptic Perspectives

In addition to physical eyesight, William Abraham suggested humanity's theological anthropology includes a spiritual eyesight—what he called the *oculus contemplationis*.[1] It is this contemplative eye that permits us to "perceive a divine order in the universe."[2] Revelation engages that spiritual sense—even as it overloads the physical sense—by incessantly offering alternate perspectives on what we see.

Revelation lays before us plenty of visuals, but it also uncovers a spiritual dimension overlooked by materialist cultures. Famines, earthquakes, wars, death, instability, chaos, and so on are all plainly visible and familiar

---

1. Abraham, *Crossing the Threshold*, 58–78.
2. Abraham, *Crossing the Threshold*, 69.

to us. But Revelation does more that attest to the existence of such calamities. Instead, it relocates them within God's mission of redemption that removes evil through Jesus' victory over sin. Revelation also offers glimpses into the heavenly alternatives to these problems by showing creation gathered around God's throne engaged in worship.

When we apply this alternate apocalyptic perspective to the life of the church, we find that the struggles we face day-to-day are more than trivial obstacles in the humdrum of life (this is especially true for comfortable Christians in places like North America and Laodicea). To the contrary, our trials are opportunities to enact faithfulness to the Lamb by following wherever he leads. Other times, the perspective of Revelation teaches that what might appear to be an inconsequential compromise is in actuality nothing less than idolatry because it diverts worship and allegiance away from Jesus. Revelation uncovers this spiritual reality while calling the people of God to awake.

2. New Exodus

Of course, Revelation is much more than a clarion call sounded to waken Jesus' sleepy followers. Having awoken, we hear the summons of Christ to a new exodus. To those in Babylon, Jesus calls, "Come out of her, my people!" (Rev 18:4). This new exodus has nothing to do with geography and everything to do with worship. Revelation summons the church to Jesus on the heavenly side of the glassy sea where we worship the one who sits on the throne.

Revelation issues this call out of Babylon—whether Rome of John's time or one of the many nations God's people have inhabited since the first century—because it knows that our world is not simply a political one; it is also a worshiping world. Revelation is about worship and its apocalyptic perspective on our world highlights the efforts of empires and other assorted beasts to deflect worship away from Jesus. That ability of Revelation to uncover the connection between civics and politics on the one hand and religious practice on the other hand leads Michael Gorman to label Revelation a *theopolitical* text.[3] Having revealed the connection between civics and religion, Revelation invites us to an "uncivil" religion that devotes allegiance to Jesus exclusively, not Jesus and somebody or something

---

3. Gorman, *Reading Revelation Responsibly*, 31–60.

else.[4] This is nothing less than a call to exodus by leaving behind religion contaminated by political interests.

3. Where Shall We Go? Faithful Worship

Of course, the question raised by any exodus is "if we leave this place, where shall we go?" Leaving Egypt is much easier than entering the promised land. Often, God's people recognize the danger of our environment, leave it, and subsequently wander around in the wilderness. In that environment, we forget how bad Egypt (or Babylon, or Rome, etc.) was and we feel the lure back into the arms of what Revelation portrayed as a prostitute. Such a return occasions the warnings Revelation issues to unfaithful Christians, lest we share in Babylon's demise.

Revelation, does not only call us *out*; it calls us *to* . . . to Jesus and to faithful worship. The victorious faithful are not those who simply depart Rome; they are the ones who follow the Lamb wherever he goes (Rev 14:4). Often, that following looks like crucifixion. It looks like defeat. It will appear there is no possible way that this could be the path to victory. And that appearance would be correct were it not for the truth Revelation proclaims: the power of the God for salvation arrives in the faithfulness of Jesus to launch God's plan of redemption. In that plan, Jesus endured the cross as the path toward a victorious resurrection. The church follows that path. The Spirit-empowered life of a witness about Jesus resembles the slaughtered but living Lamb.

Revelation issues a bold call to faithful Christlikeness and worship. Jesus calls his bride to himself. The path to him is treacherous and dangerous. Many of the faithful will die for their witness about Jesus while they follow him. Even so, Revelation bolsters the faith of these saints by offering the picture of all God's people reunited with him in the new creation. In that creation, we are welcomed into the wedding feast of the Lamb as his bride, adorned in fine wedding clothes that are the righteous acts of the saints (Rev 19:8). May God grant that in this magnificent feast, he will find us to be properly attired (Matt 22:1–14).

---

4. Gorman, *Reading Revelation Responsibly*, 176–80.

Appendix A: The Shepherd of Hermas

Excerpts from Visions 3–4

1. Introduction

The Shepherd of Hermas is a second century Christian apocalyptic writing. Although it was not included in the New Testament, many early Christians found it useful, including such notable figures as Eusebius, Jerome, and Athanasius.

As we observed in chapter 1, apocalyptic works are set within a narrative frame. For the Shepherd of Hermas, that narrative centers on the book's titular character: a man named Hermas. "The Shepherd" refers to an angel Hermas met who gave him instructions to convey to the church. There is ongoing debate regarding when Hermas might have lived. Some associate him with the man of that name in Rom 16:14. Another Christian document—the Muratorian Canon—claims Hermas was the brother of Pius, who was active in Rome in the mid-second century.[1]

Regardless of *when* Hermas might have lived, we may be relatively certain regarding *where* the experiences reported in the book transpired. Geographical references within the Shepherd of Hermas demonstrate familiarity with the vicinity of Rome. That is the book's probable point of origin, though the author certainly knew the surrounding rural area as well.

The Shepherd of Hermas divides into three large sections. The first part of the book contains five visions in which Hermas encounters a lady

---

1. See Osiek, *Shepherd of Hermas*, 5–6, 18–20.

APPENDIX A: THE SHEPHERD OF HERMAS

who symbolizes the church. In vision 5, Hermas encounters the "Shepherd," a heavenly agent who guides him and reveals the remainder of the book's content. This final vision also introduces the second and third parts of the book: twelve mandates that provide instruction for Christian faith and virtue, and ten parables (sometimes called similitudes).

The excerpts below contain Hermas's third and fourth visions. In vision 3, Hermas witnessed the construction of a large tower that represented the church. The stones used in the construction of the tower symbolized different types of Christians. In vision 4, Hermas walked along a rural road and encountered a hideous beast coming toward him. The beast symbolized a coming tribulation that would test many Christians.

The text of these excerpts comes from volume 2 of the Ante-Nicene Fathers series (ANF). I have made some adaptations to the translation to assist modern readers. These adaptations are limited to minor linguistic updates (grammar, punctuation, and some vocabulary) and are based on the Greek text in Michael Holmes's *The Apostolic Fathers*.[2] The original capitalization style of the ANF translation has been left intact, as have sentences that require more than minor updates to modernize the language. Chapter numbers found in the ANF translation have been removed to assist with the flow of the excerpts. The headings below are my own. The excerpt of vision 3 includes material from chapters 1–5 and chapter 9 in the ANF text. The excerpt of vision 4 contains the entire episode (chapters 1–3 in ANF).

2. Third Vision[3]

Prior to this point, Hermas had received two visions of the church already. We do not know how much time elapsed between the second and third visions. The text only says that prior to the third vision Hermas had been fasting and praying to God to receive a revelation that God had promised to show him.

Hermas Sees a Tower

The vision which I saw, my brethren, was of the following nature. Having fasted frequently, and having prayed to the Lord that He would show me

---

2. Holmes, "ΠΟΙΜΗΝ," 334–369.
3. Crombie, "Pastor of Hermas," vis. 3 (ANF 2:1–14).

APPENDIX A: THE SHEPHERD OF HERMAS

the revelation which He promised to show me through that old woman, the same night that old woman appeared to me, and said to me,[4]

"Since you are so anxious and eager to know all things, go into the part of the country where you tarry; and about the fifth hour I shall appear unto you, and show you all that you ought to see."

I asked her, saying "Lady, into what part of the country am I to go?"

And she said, "Into any part you wish."

Then I chose a spot which was suitable, and retired. Before, however, I began to speak and to mention the place, she said to me, "I will come where you wish."

Accordingly, I went to the country, and counted the hours, and reached the place where I had promised to meet her. And I [saw][5] an ivory seat ready placed, and on it a linen cushion, and above the linen cushion was spread a covering of fine linen. Seeing these laid out, and yet no one in the place, I began to feel awe, and as it were a trembling seized hold of me, and my hair stood on end, and as it were a horror came upon me when I saw that I was all alone. But on coming back to myself and calling to mind the glory of God, I took courage, bent my knees, and again confessed my sins to God as I had done before. Whereupon the old woman approached, accompanied by six young men whom I had also seen before; and she stood behind me, and listened to me, as I prayed and confessed my sins to the Lord. And touching me she said, "Hermas, cease praying continually for your sins; pray for righteousness, that you may have a portion of it immediately in your house."

On this, she took me up by the hand, and brought me to the seat, and said to the young men, "Go and build. . . ."

. . . And lifting up a splendid rod, she said to me, "Do you see something great?"

And I said, "Lady, I see nothing."

She said to me, "Lo! do you not see opposite to you a great tower, built upon the waters, of splendid square stones?"

For the tower was built square by those six young men who had come with her. But myriads of men were carrying stones to it, some dragging them from the depths, others removing them from the land, and they handed them to these six young men. They were taking them and building;

---

4. In order to assist readability, I have added paragraph divisions throughout this appendix that are not found in ANF.

5. Author's translations based on Holmes, *Apostolic Fathers*.

and those, of the stones that were dragged out of the depths, they placed in the building just as they were: for they were polished and fitted exactly into the other stones, and became so united one with another that the lines of juncture could not be perceived. And in this way the building of the tower looked as if it were made out of one stone. Those stones, however, which were taken from the earth suffered a different fate; for the young men rejected some of them, some they fitted into the building, and some they cut down, and cast far away from the tower. Many other stones, however, lay around the tower, and the young men did not use them in building; for some of them were rough, others had cracks in them, others had been made too short, and others were white and round, but did not fit into the building of the tower. Moreover, I saw other stones thrown far away from the tower, and falling into the public road; yet they did not remain on the road, but were rolled into a pathless place. And I saw others falling into the fire and burning, others falling close to the water, and yet not capable of being rolled into the water, though they wished to be rolled down, and to enter the water.

Hermas Inquires about the Meaning of the Vision

On showing me these visions, she wished to retire. I said to her, "What is the use of my having seen all this, while I do not know what it means?"

She said to me, "You are a cunning fellow, wishing to know everything that relates to the tower."

"Even so, O Lady," [I said,] "that I may tell it to my brethren, that, hearing this, they may know the Lord in much glory."

And she said, "Many indeed shall hear, and hearing, some shall be glad, and some shall weep. But even these, if they hear and repent, shall also rejoice. Hear, then, the parables of the tower; for I will reveal all to you, and give me no more trouble in regard to revelation: for these revelations have an end, for they have been completed. But you will not cease praying for revelations, for you are shameless. The tower which you see building is myself, the Church, who have appeared to you now and on the former occasion. Ask, then, whatever you like in regard to the tower, and I will reveal it to you, that you may rejoice with the saints."

I said unto her, "Lady, since you have vouchsafed to reveal all to me this once, reveal it."

She said to me, "Whatsoever ought to be revealed, will be revealed; only let your heart be with God, and doubt not whatsoever you shall see."

I asked her, "Why was the tower built upon the waters, O Lady?"

She answered, "I told you before, and you still inquire carefully: therefore inquiring you shall find the truth. Hear then why the tower is built upon the waters. It is because your life has been, and will be, saved through water. For the tower was founded on the word of the almighty and glorious Name, and it is kept together by the invisible power of the Lord."

The Woman Explains Those Carrying the Stones

In reply I said to her, "This is magnificent and [marvelous]. But who are the six young men who are engaged in building?"

And she said, "These are the holy angels of God, who were first created, and to whom the Lord handed over His whole creation, that they might increase and build up and rule over the whole creation. By these will the building of the tower be finished."

"But who are the other persons who are engaged in carrying the stones?"

"These also are holy angels of the Lord, but the former six are more excellent than these. The building of the tower will be finished, and all will rejoice together around the tower, and they will glorify God, because the tower is finished."

I asked her, saying, "Lady, I should like to know what became of the stones, and what was meant by the various kinds of stones?"

In reply she said to me, "Not because you are more deserving than all others that this revelation should be made to you—for there are others before you, and better than you, to whom these visions should have been revealed—but [so] that the name of God may be glorified . . . has the revelation been made to you, and it will be made on account of the doubtful who ponder in their hearts whether these things will be or not. Tell them that all these things are true, and that none of them is beyond the truth. All of them are firm and sure, and established on a strong foundation."

The Meaning of the Stones

"Hear now with regard to the stones which are in the building. Those square white stones which fitted exactly into each other, are apostles, bishops, teachers, and deacons, who have lived in godly purity, and have acted as bishops and teachers and deacons chastely and reverently to the elect of God. Some of them have fallen asleep, and some still remain alive. And they have always agreed with each other, and been at peace among themselves, and listened to each other. On account of this, they join exactly into the building of the tower."

"But who are the stones that were dragged from the depths, and which were laid into the building and fitted in with the rest of the stones previously placed in the tower?"

"They are those who suffered for the Lord's sake."

"But I wish to know, O Lady, who are the other stones which were carried from the land."

"Those," she said, "which go into the building without being polished, are those whom God has approved of, for they walked in the straight ways of the Lord and [practiced] His commandments."

"But who are those who are in the act of being brought and placed in the building?"

"They are those who are young in faith and are faithful. But they are admonished by the angels to do good, for no iniquity has been found in them."

"Who then are those whom they rejected and cast away?"

"These are they who have sinned, and wish to repent. On this account they have not been thrown far from the tower, because they will yet be useful in the building, if they repent. Those then who are to repent, if they do repent, will be strong in faith, if they now repent while the tower is building. For if the building be finished, there will not be more room for any one, but he will be rejected. This privilege, however, will belong only to him who has now been placed near the tower. . . ."

Hermas Instructs the Church

Give ear unto me, O Sons: I have brought you up in much simplicity, and guilelessness, and chastity, on account of the mercy of the Lord, who has dropped His righteousness down upon you, that [you] may be made righteous and [sanctified] from all your iniquity and depravity; but you do not wish to rest from your iniquity.

Now, therefore, listen to me, and be at peace one with another, and visit each other, and bear each other's burdens, and do not partake of

God's creatures alone, but give abundantly of them to the needy. For some through the abundance of their food produce weakness in their flesh, and thus corrupt their flesh; while the flesh of others who have no food is corrupted, because they have not sufficient nourishment [and] their bodies waste away. This intemperance in eating is thus injurious to you who have abundance and do not distribute among those who are needy. Give heed to the judgment that is to come. [You], therefore, who are high in position, seek out the hungry as long as the tower is not yet finished; for after the tower is finished, you will wish to do good, but will find no opportunity. Give heed, therefore, [you] who glory in your wealth, lest those who are needy should groan, and their groans should ascend to the Lord, and [you] be shut out with all your goods beyond the gate of the tower.

[Now, therefore,] I say to you who preside over the Church and love the first seats, "Be not like [the] drug-mixers. For the drug-mixers carry their drugs in boxes, but [you] carry your drug and poison in your heart. [You] are hardened, and do not wish to cleanse your hearts, and to add unity of aim to purity of heart, that you may have mercy from the great King. Take heed, therefore, children, that these dissensions of yours do not deprive you of your life. How will you instruct the elect of the Lord, if you yourselves have not instruction? Instruct each other therefore, and be at peace among yourselves, that I also, standing joyful before your Father, may give an account of you all to your Lord."

3. Fourth Vision[6]

Hermas Encounters a Beast

Twenty days after the former vision I saw another vision, brethren—a representation of the tribulation that is to come. I was going to a country house along the Campanian road. Now the house lay about ten furlongs from the public road. The district is one rarely traversed. And as I walked alone, I prayed the Lord to complete the revelations which He had made to me through His holy Church, that He might strengthen me and give repentance to all His servants who were going astray, that His great and glorious name might be glorified because He [regarded me worthy] to show me His marvels.

---

6. Crombie, "Pastor of Hermas," vis. 4 (ANF 2:17–18).

And while I was glorifying Him and giving Him thanks, a voice, as it were, answered me, "Doubt not, Hermas[.]"

[And] I began to think with myself, and to say, "What reason have I to doubt—I who have been established by the Lord, and who have seen such glorious sights?"

I advanced a little, brethren, and, lo! I [saw] dust rising even to the heavens. I began to say to myself, "Are cattle approaching and raising the dust?" It was about a furlong's distance from me. And, lo! I [saw] the dust rising more and more, so that I imagined that it was something sent from God.

But the sun now shone out a little, and, lo! I [saw] a mighty beast like a whale, and out of its mouth fiery locusts proceeded. But the size of that beast was about a hundred feet, and it had a head like an urn. I began to weep, and to call on the Lord to rescue me from it.

Then I remembered the word which I had heard, "Doubt not, O Hermas."

Clothed, therefore, my brethren, with faith in the Lord, and remembering the great things which He had taught me, I boldly faced the beast. Now that beast came on with such noise and force, that it could itself have destroyed a city. I came near it, and the monstrous beast stretched itself out on the ground, and showed nothing but its tongue, and did not stir at all until I had passed by it. Now the beast had four [colors] on its head—black, then fiery and bloody, then golden, and lastly white.

Hermas Meets the Lady Church

Now after I had passed by the wild beast, and had moved forward about thirty feet, lo! a virgin [met] me, adorned as if she were proceeding from the bridal chamber[. She was] clothed entirely in white, and with white sandals, and veiled up to her forehead, and her head was covered by a hood. And she had white hair.

I knew from my former visions that this was the Church, and I became more joyful. She saluted me, and said, "Hail, O man!"

And I returned her salutation, and said, "Lady, hail!"

[When she answered, she said] to me, "Has nothing crossed your path?"

I [said], "I was met by a beast of such a size that it could destroy peoples, but through the power of the Lord and His great mercy I escaped from it."

"Well did you escape from it," she [said], "because you cast your care on God, and opened your heart to the Lord, believing that you can be saved by no other than by His great and glorious name. On this account the Lord has sent His angel, who has rule over the beasts—and whose name is Thegri—and has shut up its mouth, so that it cannot tear you. You have escaped from great tribulation on account of your faith, and because you did not doubt in the presence of such a beast.

"Go, therefore, and tell the elect of the Lord His mighty deeds, and say to them that this beast is a type of the great tribulation that is coming. If then [you] prepare yourselves, and repent with all your heart, and turn to the Lord, it will be possible for you to escape it, if your heart be pure and spotless, and [you] spend the rest of the days of your life in serving the Lord blamelessly. Cast your cares upon the Lord, and He will direct them.

"Trust the Lord, [you] who doubt, for He is all-powerful, and can turn His anger away from you, and send scourges on the doubters. Woe to those who hear these words, and despise them: better were it for them not to have been born."

The Beast Explained

I asked her about the four [colors] which the beast had on his head. And she answered, and said to me, "Again you are inquisitive in regard to such matters."

"[Yes], Lady," [I said], "make known to me what they are."

"Listen," [she said,] "the black is the world in which we dwell, but the fiery and bloody points out that the world must perish through blood and fire[. Now] the golden part [is all of] you who have escaped from this world. For as gold is tested by fire, and thus becomes useful, so are you tested who dwell in it. Those, therefore, who continue [steadfast], and are put through the fire, will be purified by means of it. For as gold casts away its dross, so also will [you] cast away all sadness and [anguish], and will be made pure so as to fit into the building of the tower.

"[Now] the white part is the age that is to come, in which the elect of God will dwell, since those elected by God to eternal life will be spotless and pure. [Therefore,] cease not speaking these things into the ears of the saints. This then is the type of the great tribulation that is to come. If [you] wish it, it will be nothing. Remember those things which were written down before."

And saying this, she departed. But I [did not see] into what place she retired. There was a noise, however, and I turned around in alarm, thinking that that beast was coming.

Bibliography

Abraham, William. *Crossing the Threshold of Divine Revelation*. Grand Rapids: Eerdmans, 2006.
Aland, Barabara, et al., eds. *Novum Testamentum Graece*. 28th Revised Edition. Stuttgart: Deutsche Bibelgesellschaft, 2012. Accessed using Accordance Bible Software.
"The Apocalypse of Peter." In *The Gospel of Peter, the Diatessaron of Tatian, the Apocalypse of Peter, the Visio Pauli, the Apocalypses of the Virgil and Sedrach, the Testament of Abraham, the Acts of Xanthippe and Polyxena, the Narrative of Zosimus, the Apology of Aristides, the Epistles of Clement (Complete Text), Origen's Commentary on John, Books I-X, and Commentary on Matthew, Books I, II, and X-XIV*, edited by Allan Menzies, 145–48. ANF 9. New York: Christian Literature Company, 1897. Accessed using Logos Bible Software.
Aune, David. *Revelation 6–16*. Word Biblical Commentary. Vol. 52B. Dallas: Word, 1998.
Babcock, Maltbie. "This Is My Father's World." In *Sing to the Lord*, edited by Ken Bible, hymn 75. Kansas City: Lillenas, 1993.
Bauckham, Richard. *Theology of the Book of Revelation*. New Testament Theology. Cambridge: Cambridge University Press, 1993.
Beale, Gregory. *The Book of Revelation: A Commentary on the Greek Text*. New International Greek Testament Commentary. Grand Rapids: Eerdmans, 1999.
Beale, Gregory, and David Campbell. *Revelation: A Shorter Commentary*. Grand Rapids: Eerdmans, 2015.
Boeckel, Peter. "Saving Rest: A Biblical Theological Investigation of Sabbath." *Wesleyan Theological Journal* 56 (2020) 215–30.
Bonhoeffer, Dietrich. *The Cost of Discipleship*. New York: Touchstone, 1995.
Boring, Eugene. *Revelation*. Interpretation: A Bible Commentary for Teaching and Preaching. Louisville: Westminster John Knox, 1989.
Bridges, Matthew. "Crown Him with Many Crowns." In *Sing to the Lord*, edited by Ken Bible, hymn 272. Kansas City: Lillenas, 1993.
Caird, George. *The Revelation of St. John the Divine*. Harper's New Testament Commentaries. New York: Harper & Row, 1966.
Chapman, David W. "The Crucifixion in Paul." Bible Odyssey, n.d. https://www.bibleodyssey.org/articles/the-crucifixion-in-paul/.
Collins, John. "Introduction: Toward the Morphology of a Genre." *Semeia* 14 (1979) 1–20.

Crombie, F., translator. "The Pastor of Hermas." In *Fathers of the Second Century: Hermas, Tatian, Athenagoras, Theophilus, and Clement of Alexandria (Entire)*, edited by Alexander Roberts et al., 1–58. ANF 2. Buffalo: Christian Literature Company, 1885. Accessed using Logos Bible Software.

DeSilva, David. *Discovering Revelation: Content, Interpretation, Reception*. Grand Rapids: Eerdmans, 2021.

Gorman, Michael. *Reading Revelation Responsibly: Uncivil Worship and Witness Following the Lamb into the New Creation*. Eugene: Cascade, 2011.

Hamilton, Victor. *Exodus: An Exegetical Commentary*. Grand Rapids: Baker, 2011.

Handel, George Frederick. "Hallelujah Chorus." Hymnary, n.d. https://hymnary.org/text/hallelujah_hallelujah_for_the_lord_god_o.

Holmes, Michael William. *The Apostolic Fathers: Greek Texts and English Translations*. Grand Rapids: Baker, 1999.

———. "ΠΟΙΜΗΝ." In *The Apostolic Fathers: Greek Texts and English Translations*, 334–369. Grand Rapids: Baker, 1999.

Integrity Music. "Revelation Song—Kari Jobe (Official Live Video)." YouTube, Aug 11, 2009. https://www.youtube.com/watch?v=8-Gxjtd6Wp4.

Koester, Craig. *Revelation and the End of All Things*. Grand Rapids: Eerdmans, 2001.

Lewis, C. S. *The Silver Chair*. New York: HarperCollins, 1981.

Liddell, Henry George, et al. "Δικαίωμα." In LSJ, 429. Oxford: Clarendon, 1996.

———. "Ἶρις." In LSJ, 836. Oxford: Clarendon, 1996.

Majeski, Kimberly. "Eschatology." In *Global Wesleyan Encyclopedia of Biblical Theology*, edited by Robert Branson, 117–30. Kansas City: Beacon Hill 2020.

Mathewson, David. *Revelation: A Handbook on the Greek Text*. Waco, TX: Baylor University Press, 2016.

Metzger, Bruce. *A Textual Commentary on the Greek New Testament*. Stuttgart: German Bible Society, 1994.

Morales, L. Michael. *Who Shall Ascend the Mountain of the Lord? A Biblical Theology of the Book of Leviticus*. New Studies in Biblical Theology. Downers Grove, IL: InterVarsity, 2015.

Morris, Lelia. "Called Unto Holiness." In *Sing to the Lord*, edited by Ken Bible, hymn 503. Kansas City: Lillenas, 1993.

Mounce, Bill. *The Book of Revelation*. Rev. ed. New International Commentary on the New Testament. Grand Rapids: Eerdmans, 1997.

Osiek, Carolyn. *The Shepherd of Hermas: A Commentary*. Hermeneia. Minneapolis: Fortress, 1999.

Pelosi, Nancy. "Remarks Upon Reconvening of the House of Representatives." Representative Nancy Pelosi, Jan 6, 2021. https://pelosi.house.gov/news/press-releases/pelosi-remarks-upon-reconvening-of-the-house-of-representatives.

Rabinowitz, Louis Isaac. "Sea, Song of The." In *EncJud*, edited by Fred Skolnik and Michael Berenbaum, 14:1070–71. Detroit: Macmillan Reference USA, 2007.

Reawaken Hymns. "Holy Holy Holy | Reawaken Hymns | Official Lyric Video." YouTube, Feb 21, 2022. https://www.youtube.com/watch?v=1bk28-_xyK4.

Reddish, Mitchell. *Revelation*. Smyth & Helwys Bible Commentary. Macon, GA: Smyth & Helwys, 2001.

Robinson, Robert. "Come, Though Fount of Every Blessing." In *Sing to the Lord*, edited by Ken Bible, hymn 51. Kansas City: Lillenas, 1993.

Smith, Michael W. "Agnus Dei (Live)." YouTube, Nov 6, 2014. https://www.youtube.com/watch?v=CLCmRpj7D-w.

Sweeney, Marvin. *I and II Kings*. Old Testament Library. Louisville: Westminster, 2007.

Volf, Miroslav. *Exclusion and Embrace: A Theological Exploration of Identity, Otherness, and Reconciliation*. Nashville: Abingdon, 2019.

Walton, John. *The Lost World of Genesis One: Ancient Cosmology and the Origins Debate*. Downers Grove: IVP Academic, 2009.

Webster, Douglas. *Follow the Lamb: A Pastoral Approach to the Revelation*. Eugene: Cascade, 2014.

Wesley, Charles. "And Can It Be?" In *Sing to the Lord*, edited by Ken Bible, hymn 225. Kansas City: Lillenas, 1993.

Wesley, John. *Explanatory Notes Upon the New Testament*. London: Epworth, 1976.

Wright, N. T. *Revelation for Everyone*. Louisville: Westminster John Knox, 2011.